WORKBOOK

BOUNDARIES
in Dating

Resources by Henry Cloud and John Townsend

Boundaries
Boundaries Workbook
Boundaries *audio*
Boundaries *video curriculum*
Boundaries in Dating
Boundaries in Dating Workbook
Boundaries in Dating *audio*
Boundaries in Marriage
Boundaries in Marriage Workbook
Boundaries in Marriage *audio*
Boundaries with Kids
Boundaries with Kids Workbook
Boundaries with Kids *audio*
Changes That Heal (Cloud)
Changes That Heal Workbook (Cloud)
Changes That Heal *audio* (Cloud)
Hiding from Love (Townsend)
The Mom Factor
The Mom Factor Workbook
The Mom Factor *audio*
Raising Great Kids
Raising Great Kids for Parents of Preschoolers *curriculum*
Raising Great Kids Workbook for Parents of Preschoolers
Raising Great Kids *audio*
Safe People
Safe People Workbook
Safe People *audio*
Twelve "Christian" Beliefs That Can Drive You Crazy

WORKBOOK

BOUNDARIES
in Dating

Dr. Henry Cloud & Dr. John Townsend
with Lisa Guest

Zondervan Publishing House
Grand Rapids, Michigan

A Division of HarperCollinsPublishers

Boundaries in Dating Workbook
Copyright © 2000 by Henry Cloud and John Townsend

Requests for information should be addressed to:

⌂ ZondervanPublishingHouse
Grand Rapids, Michigan 49530

ISBN: 0-310-23330-5

Published in association with Yates & Greer, LLP, Literary Agent, Orange, CA.

Interior design by Laura Klynstra Blost

Printed in the United States of America

00 01 02 03 04 05 /❖ DC/ 10 9 8 7 6 5 4 3 2 1

CONTENTS

WHY DATING?

"Dr. Cloud, what is the biblical position on dating?" At first, I thought I had misheard the question. But the same question kept coming up around the country whenever I spoke to singles. Questions about dating were asked in response to a movement arising from the book *I Kissed Dating Good-bye* by Joshua Harris. We strongly disagree with the idea that all people should give up dating, but we certainly understand the reasons behind the movement.

- Pain, disillusionment, and detrimental effects to one's spiritual life are three valid reasons for being disillusioned with dating. Which of these three, if any, have you experienced in your own dating life, seen someone else experience, or feel concerned about for yourself as you consider dating?

- This is a good time to ask why you picked up this book. What prompted you to start reading *Boundaries in Dating*, and what do you hope to learn from it?

We don't think that dating is the problem. We think people are. In the same way that cars don't kill people, drunk drivers do, dating does not hurt people, but dating in out-of-control ways does.

- What behaviors and patterns come to mind when you hear the phrase "dating in out-of-control ways"?

- What problems with people rather than problems with the practice of dating do those behaviors and patterns you just listed indicate?

Avoiding dating isn't the way to cure the problems encountered in dating. The cure is the same as the Bible's cure for all of life's problems, and that is *spiritual growth leading to maturity*. Learning how to love, follow God, be honest and responsible, treat others as you want to be treated, develop self-control, and build a fulfilling life will ensure better dating.

- Turn to pages 14–15 of *Boundaries in Dating* and review the list of "negative tendencies" from Joshua Harris's chapter "The Seven Habits of Highly Defective Dating." Which, if any, of these "tendencies" in a person you have dated has caused you pain, disillusionment, or other detrimental effects?

- Which of these seven tendencies, if any, have you yourself fallen into in any dating you've done? (We'll be addressing each one of these problems so that history won't repeat itself.)

All of the problem scenarios listed are created by people and the way that they date. In each case, the underlying issue is the lack of appropriate structure within, among other things, a person's character, support system, values, and relationship with God. In other words, a lack of *boundaries,* and that is a character issue, a people problem.

- At this point, what do you understand about boundaries? (We'll define this more thoroughly in chapter 1. For a comprehensive discussion of the concept, read our book *Boundaries*.)

- The lack of appropriate structure, the lack of boundaries, is a maturity problem. The situations Harris builds his kiss-dating-good-bye case on are caused by the immaturity of the people involved. But Harris's logic seems to be Person A dated Person B; Person A or B or both got hurt; dating is bad. This is a little like saying because there are car accidents, no one should drive.

—When have you, if ever, grown from and been grateful for a dating experience? Be specific about how you benefited.

—Not dating is a good idea for a few people. When, if ever, have you fallen into that category? Explain your answer.

—In your opinion, what signs of maturity indicate a readiness to date? Are you ready to date?

We think dating can be a very good experience. Consider now a few of the benefits we see in dating. (If you haven't dated and can't yet share from your own experience, questions here and throughout the workbook will give you some important things to think about.)

1. Dating gives people the opportunity to learn about themselves, others, and relationships in a safe context.

—What have you learned—or do you expect to learn—about yourself in a dating relationship?

—What have you learned—or do you expect to learn—about other people from dating relationships?

—What context makes dating "safe"? (Hint: Community!)

2. Dating provides a context to work through issues.

—When have you been surprised once you moved on from an initial impression and got to know better the person you were dating? Explain.

—What have you learned—or do you expect to learn—from dating about what you value in a person for the long term?

3. Dating helps build relationship skills.

—What insecurities in yourself, if any, has your dating helped you recognize?

—What lack of certain relationship skills have you realized as you've dated? Consider communication, vulnerability, trust, assertiveness, honesty, self-sacrifice, and listening.

4. Dating can heal and repair.

—When have you seen or experienced for yourself dating as a place of learning, healing, and growth even if that relationship didn't lead to marriage?

—Dating is a place where good things happen in people's souls. Name one or two good things that you've experienced—or hope to experience—in dating.

5. Dating is relational and has value in and of itself.

—Why is relationship valuable? See, for instance, Genesis 2:18, Ecclesiastes 4:9–12, Galatians 6:2, and Hebrews 10:24–25.

—As you've dated, whom have you simply enjoyed getting to know even though the relationship didn't lead to marriage? Each name you list is an argument *for* dating!

6. Dating lets someone learn what he or she likes in the opposite sex.

—What we sometimes think we like is not what would really be good for us long term, but we have to find this out. When have you seen this truth played out or perhaps experienced it yourself? Be specific about the lesson learned.

—Dating enables people to find out what they like, what they need, and what is good for them in another person. Thanks to your dating, what discoveries, if any, have you made in each of these three categories.

What you like in another person—

What you need in another person—

What is good for you in another person—

7. Dating gives a context to learn sexual self-control and other delay of gratification.

—Why are sexual self-control and other delay of gratification essential in dating?

—Why are sexual self-control and other delay of gratification essential in marriage?

Dating can be done poorly and can lead to hurt and pain. Dating can be done well and can lead to wonderful fruits in the life of the teen and the adult single. If you take this book seriously, seek God as deeply as you know how, establish a healthy community of friends to support you in the process, keep God's boundaries for living a fulfilled, but holy life, then dating can be something wonderful indeed.

For dating to be a great time of life, it must be balanced with God's boundaries of what is good. We hope *Boundaries in Dating* helps you find that safety, fulfillment, growth, and freedom.

HENRY CLOUD, PH.D.
JOHN TOWNSEND, PH.D.

Part One

YOU AND YOUR BOUNDARIES

Chapter I

Why Boundaries in Dating?

Heather had made Todd a high emotional priority in her life. She had given up activities she enjoyed; she had given up relationships she valued. She had tried to become the kind of person she thought Todd would be attracted to. And now it looked like this investment was going nowhere.

No Kids Allowed (page 26)[1]

Though dating has its difficulties, we believe in dating. We think it offers lots of good things, such as, for starters, opportunities to grow personally and learn how to relate to people.

- So why do we say, "No kids allowed"?

We don't believe that teens should not date. Rather, teens who can take appropriate ownership of their lives can enjoy and benefit from dating.

- Dating works best between two responsible people. What can happen when one party is irresponsible?

Dating does have its risks. That's why the maturity of the two people involved is very important.

---

[1] The subtitles and page numbers refer to corresponding sections and pages in the book *Boundaries in Dating*.

—What problems can arise in a dating relationship if you're not taking responsibility to speak the truth in love, to protect love by confronting problems (Ephesians 4:15)? Give a real-life example or two.

- Freedom and responsibility create a safe and secure environment for a couple to love, trust, explore, and deepen their experience of each other. What relationship that you've been involved in—or that you're aware of—would freedom and responsibility have improved or cured? Explain.

Before we take a look at the ways that dating problems arise from freedom and responsibility conflicts, let's take a brief look at what boundaries are and how they function in dating relationships.

What Are Boundaries? (page 28)

Let's take a look at what a boundary is, its functions and purpose, and some examples.

- *A Property Line*—Just as a physical fence marks out where your yard ends and your neighbor's begins, a personal boundary distinguishes what is your emotional or personal property and what belongs to someone else. When, if ever, have you recognized that your boundary has been crossed? Give an example or two.

- *The Functions of Boundaries*—Boundaries define us by showing what we are and are not; what we agree and disagree with; what we love and hate. Boundaries also protect us by keeping good things in and bad things out and by letting others know what we will and will not tolerate.

—What values, preferences, and morals do you want to be clear about right from the start in your dating relationships? List three or four points.

Problems in Freedom and Responsibility (page 26)

We are writing about the problems people have in how they conduct their dating lives. Simply put, many of the struggles people experience in dating relationships are, at heart, caused by some problem in the areas of freedom and responsibility.

- By freedom we mean your ability to make choices based on your values, rather than choosing out of fear, guilt, or need.

—Think about some of the choices you've recently made, ideally in a dating relationship but perhaps in a friendship or family relationship. To what degree did fear, guilt, or need motivate your choice? What did you fear, what were you feeling guilty about, what guilt were you trying to avoid, and/or what need were you trying to meet?

—What problems can arise in a dating relationship if you're making choices out of fear or guilt rather than based on your values? Give a real-life example or two.

- By responsibility, we mean your ability to execute your tasks in keeping the relationship healthy and loving, as well as being able to say no to things you shouldn't be responsible for.

—Again, think about a recent dating experience, a friendship, or a relationship with a family member. What have you done to keep the relationship healthy and loving? Be specific about one or two tasks. Also describe an opportunity you had to say no to something you shouldn't be responsible for. Be specific first about that "something." Then explain why you were or weren't able to say no and describe the consequences of your action or inaction.

—What are two or three behaviors or attitudes that you will not tolerate in a dating relationship?

• ***Examples of Boundaries***—Words, the truth, distance, and other people are four kinds of limits we can set and use in dating. Review the discussion on pages 29–30. When has one of these boundaries been helpful in a dating relationship—or when could it be? Give an example.

There are several kinds of limits we can set and use in dating, all depending on the circumstances. Whatever the situation, boundaries give you freedom and choices.

What's Inside Your Boundaries (page 30)

Remember that boundaries are a fence protecting your property. In dating, your property is your own soul: Your boundaries define and protect your love, your emotions, your values, your behaviors, and your attitudes.

• When, if ever, have you let someone else control your love, emotions, values, behaviors, or attitudes? Why did you feel unable to set limits on their control?

• When, if ever, have you been aware of controlling or trying to control another person's love, emotions, values, behaviors, or attitudes? Why did you choose to not respect his or her boundaries?

Boundaries are the key to keeping your very soul safe, protected, and growing.

How Boundary Problems Show Themselves (page 30)

There are lots of ways that dating suffers when freedom and responsibility are not appropriately present. We've listed a few of them. (They're defined on pages 31–33.)

> Loss of freedom to be oneself
> Being with the wrong person
> Dating from inner hurt rather than our values
> Not dating
> Doing too much in the relationship
> Freedom without responsibility
> Control issues
> Not taking responsibility to say no
> Sexual impropriety

- Where, if at all, do you see yourself in this list? Be honest with yourself so that you can learn and grow.

- Into which one of these nine categories has someone you've dated fit? Think about people you've dated. How did that behavior impact the relationship?

Which of these boundary problems has any of them displayed?

There are many more ways that dating can become misery because of freedom and responsibility problems. As you will see, understanding and applying boundaries in the right way can make a world of difference in how you approach the dating arena.

Before You Close the Book . . .

- Which take-away tip on page 33 do you most need to take away?

> *Lord God, thank you for what you're showing me about myself and where I can grow. Please give me both the wisdom to set good and godly boundaries in dating as well as the courage to keep them. And help me stay on this path of learning and growing. In Jesus' name. Amen.*

Chapter 2

Require and Embody Truth

*T*he wise psychiatrist taught, "As soon as there is any kind of deception, stop everything. Where there is deception there is no relationship." Truthfulness is everything. Honesty is the bedrock of dating and marriage.

Standing on Quicksand (page 36)

Remember the woman whose marriage was not ripped apart by the affair, as devastating as that was, but by the lying?

- Why is lying more destructive than the behavior that is being covered up?

- When have you been deceptive or been deceived in a relationship, dating or otherwise? What impact did that dishonesty have on the relationship?

When you are with someone who is deceptive, you never know what reality is. As one woman said, "It makes you question everything."

Deception in Dating (page 37)

There are many different ways to deceive someone in the world of dating. We've listed six of the more common ones.

- *Deception About Your Relationship*—Losing a love that one desires is almost inevitable in the dating life at some time or another, but losing one's trust in the opposite sex does not have to happen if people are honest with one another (Ephesians 4:25).

  —When, if ever, have you found yourself in Matt's position and been deceived about the relationship's significance to the other person? What did you learn from your experience or perhaps from Matt's?

  —When, if ever, have you found yourself in Karen's position and deceived a person you were dating about the relationship's significance to you? What did you learn from that experience or from this discussion of such an experience?

As soon as someone is sure that dating is not going where another person thinks or hopes it is, that person has a responsibility to tell the other one clearly and honestly. Anything less is deceitful and harmful.

- *Deception About Being Friends*—While Karen was acting like a girlfriend when in reality she was just a friend, there are those who are deceptive about their true intentions while they are acting like a friend.

  —When, if ever, has someone pretended to be a friend to you but had ulterior motives? What impact did that deception have on the "friendship"?

  —When, if ever, have you pretended to be a friend but had ulterior motives? What would have been a healthier (i.e., honest) approach?

Don't act like a friend that you are not. And only you know for sure.

- ***Deception About Other People***—Sometimes people deceive each other about the nature of other people in their lives. They may act like someone is "just a friend," when there is more of a history or more in the present than is being said.

—When, if ever, has someone you've dated been less than honest about someone in his/her life? What happened after that deception was revealed?

—When, if ever, have you been less than honest with someone about another person in your life? What statement of the truth could you have made early on? What pain (your own or someone else's) might have been avoided had you been honest?

Once a pattern of deception is begun, trust is difficult to reestablish.

- ***Deception About Who You Are***—It is important to remember that you will have a good relationship to the degree that you are able to be clear and honest about everything.

—Why do you hesitate, if you do, to be honest about everything, from the kind of ice cream you like to what you believe about God? What does your answer tell you about yourself—and what will you do to become healthier?

—Maybe you've known or dated someone who wasn't able to be honest, who hesitated even to express an opinion or make a choice. How did you respond? Why is such behavior bad for a relationship?

—When have you seen compliance (your own or someone else's) attract a controlling, self-centered person? What is unhealthy about that kind of relationship?

Be honest, have some differences, and enjoy the trip.

• ***Deception About Facts***—Some people tell lies not about feelings, relationships, or personal preferences, but about reality itself, about cold, hard, objective facts.

—When, if ever, has someone you've known or dated lied about reality? Was that deception a red flag for you? Why or why not?

—When, if ever, have you lied about reality to someone you've known or dated? Why did you do that? What impact did your dishonesty have on your relationship? What are you doing to become a person of greater integrity?

When you catch the person you are dating in any kind of lie, see that as a character issue that you should take as a very solemn warning.

• ***Deception About Hurt and Conflict***—One of the most important things you can do in a dating relationship is to be honest about hurt and conflict. Being honest enables you to resolve the hurt or conflict. And when you are honest, how the other person responds tells you whether a real, long-term, satisfactory relationship is possible. Both the Bible and relationship research are very clear: People who can handle confrontation and feedback are the ones who can make relationships work (Proverbs 9:8).

—When there is a problem with how you've been treated or when you have suffered some hurt, you must be honest. When have you opted for honesty? What happened?

And when, if ever, have you kept quiet instead of being honest? What happened in that relationship?

—What have you learned about a friend or a date during the discussion of a hurt or an attempt to resolve a conflict? Give a specific example or two. Has a person's response ever been a red flag for you? Should it have been? Why or why not?

—How do you respond when a person is honest about how you have hurt him/her or when you're trying to resolve a conflict? How would you like to respond—and what will you do to get to that point?

Being honest is totally up to you. You cannot control your date's actions. But you can decide what kind of person you are going to be, and as a result, you will also be deciding what kind of person you are going to be with.

Two Types of Liars (page 43)

In our opinion, there are two categories of liars. First, there are liars who lie out of shame, guilt, fear of conflict or loss of love, and other fears. The second category are liars who lie as a way of operating and deceive others for their own selfish ends.

- Trying to help someone in the first category learn to tell the truth is a noble goal. But why is that attempt to rehabilitate not appropriate in a dating relationship?

- Why should you run, run, run from a perpetual liar, a liar in the second category?

Lying destroys. By and large, the best policy is to stay away from those who lie for any reason. We think you should spend your time and heart on honest people.

Truth: The Essential Boundary (page 45)

We believe that truthfulness is the basis for almost anything. You should have an absolute zero-tolerance policy when it comes to deception. Lying should have no place in your life.

- We are clear, straightforward, and rigid: *Do not tolerate lying,* period. Nevertheless we understand that intimacy grows in a dating relationship, and we understand the use of a fig leaf. Explain how those points don't weaken our call to not tolerate lying.

- Again, don't tolerate deception or lying when it happens. Make a rule: "I have to be with someone who is honest with me about what they are thinking or feeling." Review the steps to take if you are lied to (page 46). What steps would be hard for you to take? Who could help you take those steps if you ever need to? Finally, review in your own mind why you should deal with lying in a relationship rather than ignore it or pretend it isn't there.

Lying is one of the most dangerous of all character problems. Do not tolerate it. Remember, to the extent that you are being deceived, there is no relationship.

You Get What You Deserve (page 47)

If you don't want to be in a relationship with a liar, be an honest person yourself.

- Are you an honest person? Explain why you've answered as you have. What evidence (including people you're in relationship with) can you point to in support of your yes or no?

- Why does being honest attract honest people rather than deceivers? Feel free to use Jesus' metaphor of light and darkness in your answer (John 3:19–21).

Be light and attract light. That is the best boundary of all.

Before You Close the Book . . .

- Which take-away tip on page 48 do you most need to take away?

Lord God, you are light and you are truth. Help me to live truthfully and to be your light in all my relationships. And help me not to be afraid to confront darkness. Give me the boldness to deal with the existence of deception when I see it and then the courage to walk away from a relationship that isn't going to be based in truth. In Jesus' name. Amen.

Chapter 3

Take God on a Date

*I*n dating, you get connected to someone you are really drawn to, and you hope against hope that God is a part of his life and of the life of the relationship. And sometimes your hope bends the realities of the situation.

- When have you bent the realities because you so wanted the person you were dating to be committed to the Lord just as you are — or when have you seen someone do this? What happened in that relationship?

It is a very good thing to want the person you are close to to also be close to God. If relationship is about connecting all of ourselves to another, then the spiritual aspect is inconceivably significant. But when we desire God and we desire a person, we sometimes don't know if the desires are working together or not. It is difficult to navigate through the spiritual dimension of dating.

- Which questions listed on page 50 have you asked? Which do you want answers to now?

As you address the issues in this chapter, you will be equipped to set boundaries which will deepen the spiritual part of your dating life.

Dating Right Side Up (page 51)

The first thing to deal with is an appropriate stance on dating and your spiritual life. The issue is not how to fit our spiritual life into our dating life; rather, it is how to fit our dating life into our spiritual life.

- Why is trying to fit our spiritual life into our dating life upside down? What can happen to one's spiritual life in such a case?

- What does fitting our dating life into our spiritual life indicate about our priorities and about the genuineness of our faith? What cost can come with dating right side up like this—and what blessings?

It is good to offer our dating life as part of the living sacrifice that helps us submit all aspects of our lives to God's order. The more our lives are surrendered to him, the more he is able to fashion our lives as they were meant to be (Acts 17:28).

Idolatry (page 51)

The alternative to surrendering our dating life to God is idolatry. We commit idolatry by demanding that dating bring us the love or fulfillment we want without allowing God to point the way.

- When have you seen a person's relationship with God waxing or waning depending on his dating relationship—or when have you experienced that yourself? What is dangerous about such a situation?

- Look again at 1 Corinthians 7:32–34. When have you experienced that truth for yourself or seen it worked out in another person's life?

Surrender brings us into proper alignment with God so that many other things can happen that will grow us up.

The Fruit of Your Dating Relationship (page 52)

When you date, it's important to ask yourself how your dating relationship impacts your spiritual life. Does it bring you closer to God, or push you further away? Important relationships rarely keep us in neutral spiritually.

- Look again at the questions for evaluating the impact your dating relationship is having on your spiritual life (pages 52–53). Why are these important to answer— and to answer honestly?

- If you are currently in a dating relationship, answer these six questions. Be honest with yourself and open to what God might have you recognize about your dating relationship.

Let's assume you've aligned yourself under the lordship of Christ. At this point, we want to look at several parts of dating and spirituality to help you define what your boundaries should be in this area.

What Needs to Grow? (page 53)

It is a great experience to begin to unveil yourself to your date spiritually. You can share deeper parts of yourself, thereby growing closer to each other and to God. Let's look at five aspects of your spiritual life that you will want to bring into the relationship.

1. Faith Story—Every believer has a story of how their relationship with God began and developed.

—What faith story do you—or could you—share with a date?

—What elements of someone else's faith story (a date's, a friend's, or a relative's) have encouraged you and drawn you closer to that person and to the Lord?

2. **Values**—Your values are the architecture of who you are. They are comprised of what you believe is most important in life and how you conduct your life in accordance with these beliefs.

—What do you believe and/or desire in the following aspects of life? Jot down two or three key points for each.

Theology
Calling in life
Relationships
Job and career
Finances
Family
Sex
Social issues

—How do you or could you make these values part of your dating world? What questions could you ask and what stances would you take?

Theology
Calling in life
Relationships
Job and career
Finances
Family
Sex
Social issues

3. **Struggles**—Failure, loss, confusion, mistakes, and learning experiences are part of the life of faith. So, to know a person's spiritual walk is also to know the times he stumbled in the darkness. If you don't know your date's spiritual struggles, you can't honestly say you know your date.

—Which of your own spiritual struggles do you need to share at an appropriate time if you want to be known in a dating relationship? (See page 56 for four possibilities.) How would you describe or explain the issue(s)?

—When, if ever, has being brought into a date's or a friend's spiritual struggle made that relationship richer, if not easier? Explain.

4. *Spiritual Autonomy*—People who are trying to pull off a successful dating relationship need to know that the other person is spiritually autonomous, that he has his own walk with God that he pursues on a regular basis, regardless of his circumstances. Spiritual autonomy also has to do with the spiritual disciplines of the faith (page 58).

—Why is it important to date (and marry!) someone who is owning his or her spiritual walk? For starters, consider Ecclesiastes 4:10.

—Why is time key to determining whether your date is truly spiritually autonomous?

5. *Friendships*—You can learn a lot about people by the sort of friends they keep. The number of Christian friends, for instance, can be a telling detail.

—What do your friendships reveal about you, your priorities, your faith, your spiritual health?

—Think of a friend or a date. What does that person's friendships reveal?

These questions about a person's spiritual condition are not meant to be tools for judgmental scrutiny. Instead, they are intended to help both you and your date to examine your hearts and your relationships with God and each other.

Differences Can Promote Growth (page 59)

The fundamentals of the Christian life are basic requirements, but we are not asking you to require your date to hold precisely the same theological or traditional values in all areas, large and small, that you do.

- What differences between your beliefs and those of a friend or a date have promoted your own spiritual growth? Be specific about the beliefs as well as the growth.

- When spiritual differences have arisen in a relationship, have you noticed in yourself or the other person any of the following: control issues, perfectionism, or uncertainty about one's faith? What growth may have resulted?

Fall in love with someone who can challenge you spiritually! Let the sparks fly and the growth follow!

Integration of Faith into Real Life (page 59)

Religious people know the Truth, but spiritual people do it. And that is what character is all about: integrating the realities of God's ordinances into everyday life.

- In what aspects of your life, if any, have you struggled to bring your spiritual values into real life? Consider, for instance, finances, sexuality, and job concerns as well as relationships (below we'll look at two forms of this struggle which take place in relationships).

1. ***Difficulties in Bringing Up Faith Matters***—You can tell a lot about character by how a person operates in the world, but character maturity is not always derived from Christian belief. So it is important to address issues of faith pretty soon.

—Why do you struggle to bring up faith matters with a new friend or a new date? See page 60 for some possible reasons.

—What everyday opportunities for bringing up faith matters with a date can you seize? What questions might you ask or statement might you make to bring up the topic of your faith in Jesus?

2. ***Difficulties in Living the Life***—The inability to integrate their needs and life into God's way of meeting needs may be the problem when people don't "walk the talk" in certain areas of their dating life.

—When, if ever, have you not walked your spiritual talk in a relationship with a date or a friend? Why do you think you struggled to do so?

—When has a date or a friend not walked the spiritual talk in a relationship with you? What did you do about that inconsistency when you noticed it—or what would you want to do in the future if such a situation arises?

—"Don't demand perfection in your date or yourself. Instead, require righteousness." Outline a dating scenario or two showing the difference between demanding perfection and demanding righteousness. Consider, for instance, addressing a person who struggles to admit mistakes or someone whose business or sexual dealings don't fit the Christian way of life. What would demanding perfection look like? How would demanding righteousness be different?

A righteous person stays connected to God, his source. And when he slips and falls, he will take correction well, reconnect to God, and work on whatever issue caused the slip.

An Active Role in Each Other's Growth (page 62)

Another aspect of the spiritual part of dating is that you need to matter to each other on a spiritual level. You need to take the stance that during your tenure as dates, you both will grow spiritually. Here are some ways two people can help each other grow.

- *Input and Feedback*—How do you want to respond to input and feedback from a date?

- *Give It Time*—What happens if we don't receive grace before we hear truth—and why is letting some time pass before confronting a friend an act of grace?

- *Don't Be a Parent*—What can you do to avoid the tendency to become spiritually responsible for your date?

- **Comfort and Challenge**—Do you more naturally challenge people or offer them comfort? Why is balance important for spiritual growth?

Spiritual Compatibility (page 64)

A major aspect of dating is spiritual compatibility, or the extent to which you are a good match in your faith lives. After all, God has designed you for intimacy with himself and others.

- **The Design Issue**—The deepest part of you is made to desire spiritual intimacy with another person. If that part of you is working properly, you will seek out healthy spirituality in others.

— What do your relationships (past and present, dating and otherwise) show about whether that part of you is working properly?

—What do your current dating relationships (if any) suggest about your own spiritual health?

- **Spiritual Development Path**—Spiritual development means that you are not who you were nor are you who you will be.

—Describe in a few words the place you are right now on your spiritual development path.

—Wherever you are on your journey, what is good advice if your date is still questioning the content and meaning of her Christianity?

• ***Areas of Belief and Practice***—As you get to know your date spiritually, you will need to decide what disagreements about belief and practice you can live with and which you can't.

—And that decision will be based on your understanding of the tenets of Christianity. How well versed are you in those? In what areas, if any, are you unclear or undecided—and what will you do to become more informed?

—When, if ever, have your date's beliefs or spiritual practices been a red flag? What is a wise course of action in such a situation?

Differences in Spiritual Level (page 66)

Many people struggle with questions about dating others who are at a different level than they are spiritually. Here are some differences. Summarize our suggestions for dealing with them and point out where, if at all, you disagree.

• ***Christian and non-Christian:***

• ***Committed and Uncommitted Christians:***

- *Mature and New Christians:*

Conclusion (page 69)

Ultimately, the spiritual part of dating means we are to set limits on all sorts of desires and impulses, some of which are listed on page 69.

- Which of those bulleted items are issues for you? Make them a topic of both prayer and awareness.

- What are you currently doing to grow in Christ and walk his paths—or what could you be doing?

As we continue to grow in Christ, it becomes easier to love and invest our hearts wisely and well in our dating lives.

Before You Close the Book . . .

- Which take-away tip on page 69 do you most need to take away?

Lord God, you do indeed want to be Lord of my life, every aspect of it. I want that too, yet I struggle to live that way. Teach me to live with you as my priority even if it costs me in my dating relationships. And grow my knowledge and love for you so that I am "walking my talk" and living with integrity a life that honors you. In Jesus' name. Amen.

Chapter 4

Dating Won't Cure a Lonely Heart

- What first came to mind when you read the title of this chapter?

- Review Marsha's experiences. At what points, if any, do you see yourself in Marsha?

- Fear of being alone might prompt us to do things that are unhealthy. Turn to page 72 and review the list of some possibilities. When, if ever, have you done one or more of these things?

- There is a very important rule in dating and romance: To be happy in a dating relationship, and to pick the kind of relationship that is going to be the kind you desire, you must be able to be happy without one.

—When have you seen this truth worked out in real life, either in your experience or in someone else's?

—Why is this truth important to recognize and live by?

- In order to cure your fear of being alone, you need to put a boundary around your wish for a dating relationship. There is nothing wrong with the desire. Just don't let it be a demand that controls you. Cure that fear first and then find a relationship. And how do you cure that fear?

—First, strengthen your relationship with God. How will you do that?

—Second, strengthen your relationships with safe, healthy Christians. Who in your life falls into that category—or where will you find safe, healthy Christians?

- You need a support system to ground you so that you can make dating choices out of strength, not weakness or dependency.

—Describe your support system—or jot down some ideas about developing a stronger one.

—In those supportive relationships, are you allowing yourself to be dependent, have needs, and express pain and hurts? Support your answer with specific examples of your vulnerability.

- A person living a full life of spiritual growth, personal growth, vocational growth, altruistic service, hobbies, and intellectual growth does not have the time or inclination to be dependent on a date. We've addressed your spiritual life. What are you doing to be active and grow in these other areas?

  Personal development
  Job/career
  Service to others
  Hobbies and recreation
  Intellectual pursuits

As you grow spiritually, you are going to naturally be closer to others and get a fuller life. The whole person is not a dating addict. He or she is happy and fulfilled. And the by-product of a full life is that the fulfilled person is also a very attractive one.

- In addition to having an active life, work on the issues that are in your soul.

—What issues (past childhood hurts, recurring themes and patterns in your relationships and work life, other areas of brokenness, pain, and dysfunction) are you or could you be addressing?

—Does your fear of aloneness pertain to a specific issue? How are you dealing with that issue—or what could you do to determine what that issue is?

The best boundary against giving in to bad relationships, less-than-satisfactory relationships, or bad dynamics in a good relationship is your not being dependent on that relationship. And that is going to come from being grounded in God, grounded in a support system, working out your issues, having a full life, and pursuing wholeness. If you are doing those things, you will be less subject to saying yes when you should be saying no.

Before You Close the Book . . .

- Which take-away tip on pages 75–76 do you most need to take away?

Heavenly Father, you know me better than I know myself. Please show me what is behind my lack of healthy boundaries—and then guide my steps toward health. Show me, too, what good things to fill my life with and where I can go to grow spiritually, personally, and intellectually; in my work, my hobbies, and my service to others. And, most of all, I ask you to help me live out the truth that I need you more than I need any other relationship. In Jesus' name. Amen.

Chapter 5

Don't Repeat the Past

*W*hen I (Dr. Townsend) asked married people what they would have done differently in their dating days, most of them told me something like, "I would have learned more from my previous mistakes." That response suggests how important it is to set a boundary with your past, that is, to deal with your old dating patterns as something that you are not destined to continue. This chapter will deal with how your past affects your dating, and what you can do to make your past work for you instead of against you.

Dating Patterns (page 78)

Become a good historian of yourself. Look for problematic patterns of dating that hinder progress toward depth, commitment, and marriage.

- Describe any problematic patterns in your dating past that you're aware of at this point of *Boundaries in Dating*. Some possibilities are the tendency to go too quickly, to adapt to your date's desires, and to allow the relationship to rule you.

- In a way, this entire book is about the various dating problems people have encountered in the past and how to deal with them. What will you do to note any patterns you can identify with as you read this book? Write a brief description of each and page reference inside the back cover? Keep a running log on a bookmark?

Once you note patterns you identify with, you can learn what to do to stop repeating the pattern.

What Can I Learn from the Past? (page 78)

The first dating problem is denying that your past demonstrates a problem! You can't learn from the past if you believe the issue is solely the unsuitable people you have dated. So spend some time wrestling with the following two questions. (A safe, honest, and long time friend might be able to help you.)

- What can I learn from my dating past that will help me avoid bad things or experience good things in the future?

- What have I done to contribute to my dating problems today?

This exercise is not about self-condemnation. Instead, it is about a quest for truth and reality, to free you up from repeating past mistakes.

Understanding the Past Helps Us to Grow (page 79)

Remember Jim? Review his story (pages 79–81) and see how he learned from his past and grew from those lessons.

- What understanding and insight did Jim gain when he looked at his dating past?

- What changes in his behavior and what risks did Jim's insight prompt him to take?

- What encouragement do you find in Jim's story?

The past's examples and warnings (1 Corinthians 10:11) proved a helpful ally for Jim. He let his insights point to some deficits and injuries in his own character and prompt some attempts at personal growth.

Be Afraid of Your Past (page 81)

Another good element of setting boundaries with your dating past is a healthy fear of the consequences of repeating the past. This fear is a healthy concern over our accountability to God for how we conduct our lives. So—be afraid, be very afraid—of the right things. Here are some of them.

- **Be Afraid of Ruining Your Present Relationship**—Don't neglect your past just because your present is good. Doing the hard work of growth now can help prevent problems in the future. If you're currently in a good dating relationship, why is that an opportune time to do some hard work of growth?

- **Be Afraid of Staying with Your Present Relationship**—You may be in a relationship that isn't so good. If that's the case, how might looking at your past help you?

- **Be Afraid of Being Injured**—Perhaps in the past you have invested in and trusted someone who was not very trustworthy. Look at that past: Why were you hurt? What tools could help prevent that hurt in the future?

- **Be Afraid of Wasting Time**—What mental time frame for marriage do you have in your mind? Why is it wise to be afraid of wasting time?

- **Be Afraid of Reducing Your Prospects**—Why does failing to learn from the past mean less freedom to be yourself? And why does this lack of freedom mean fewer prospects for healthy and potentially rewarding relationships?

We need to clearly understand the prospects we face if things remain the same as well as the risks of not learning and growing from our past. This understanding helps us bear the pain of changing.

Why the Past Still Rules (page 83)

If there are so many good reasons to work through our past dating patterns, why do people have difficulty doing so? There are several causes.

- **Lack of Maturity**—One indicator of character maturity is the ability to be aware, curious, and concerned about one's past patterns.

—What does this indicator suggest about your level of maturity?

—What evidence in your life, if any, supports the possibility that you are more interested in living only in the present than in learning from the past and growing for the future?

—What safe individuals could help you grow in love and truth? Make that process and the development of safe friendships a topic of prayer.

- ***Fear of the Unknown***—Fearing the unknown—worrying about what might happen if you change—can stall the growth process.

—Which do you prefer: a known bad thing or an unknown thing?

—Is being honest in a dating relationship an unknown thing? If so, what close friend(s) can help you practice becoming honest and direct? That practice will help the unknown become a known good thing.

- ***Fear of the Known***—Some people repeat the past because they have tried to change their patterns and suffered greatly for some reason. The pain was sufficient to stop their attempt to change.

    When, if ever, have your attempts to change and grow resulted in pain? Be specific about your attempts.

—Consider the situation(s) you just described. Were your attempts to grow being directed toward or shared with the wrong person? Were you, for instance, practicing being honest with someone who wasn't safe, someone who loved darkness instead of light (John 3:19)? Make sure your fear of the known is accurate and appropriate.

—As the old Alcoholics Anonymous saying goes, change occurs when the pain of remaining the same is greater than the pain of changing. What pain, if any, are you living with in a current relationship? What pain of changing seems worse than that pain?

• *Isolation*—One major obstacle to resolving the past is the state of being cut off from the source of life, which is relationship with God and others. Relationship is the fuel which makes change and growth possible.

—Review the description of all that relationship provides for people trying to grow and change (page 86). When, if ever, have you experienced that kind of comfort, support, or reality?

—What kind of fuel supply are you working with right now? In other words, do you have enough support to deal with the past and resolve it, to make change and growth possible? If not, where will you go for fuel?

A Final Word About the Past (page 86)

It is important to understand that you must have a past to resolve it. In other words, you need to be aware that your past dating patterns have been a problem and that today you want to change that pattern.

• Are you aware of your past . . . ? If so, ask God to guide you as you deal with it. (See the prayer below.)

- . . . Or do you seem only to be dealing with a continuous, painful present that doesn't work for you? If so, ask God to help you begin to repent of (turn from) your pattern.

Repentance creates a break between past and present, so that we may then heal from the effects of the past.

Before You Close the Book . . .

- Which take-away tip on page 87 do you most need to take away?

Eternal God, you are the same yesterday, today, and tomorrow.
You are God of the past, the present, the future. So I ask you to help me
see my dating patterns of the past, own those patterns and resolve them in
the present, and grow beyond them for the future. Lord, I look to you
and to safe relationships you'll provide me to change and be healthier
and spiritually stronger. In Jesus' name. Amen.

Part Two

WHOM SHOULD
I DATE?

Chapter 6

What You Can Live With and What You Can't Live With

*I*n this chapter, we want you to look at your "boundaries of choices." We want you to look at what your requirements are for the people you date.

- What qualities come to mind when you read the question "What do you look for in a person to date seriously or marry?"

- What was your reaction to the list of reasons people give for wanting to end their relationship (page 92)?

- What qualities in a person does that list prompt you to add to your original list?

You've taken some time to think about what you're looking for in a person you'll date. Now we want you to examine preferences that might be too limiting; preferences that you should value; minor imperfections you might have to learn to deal with; and major imperfections that you should never have to live with.

Limiting Preferences (page 93)

What about preferences? Shouldn't people have tastes and desires in what they are look-ing for in people to date? Sure you should. It's all part of knowing who you are and what you like and don't like.

- Remember the young man whose preferences were contradictory, who, for instance, wanted a hard-driver in business and a stay-at-home mom? If you haven't already, make a list of your preferences and then look for any contradictions.

- ***Surprises Happen***—Know your tastes and what is important to you, but stay open and flexible in dating, for you never know what might happen.

—Sheila was surprised that she married Jason. When, if ever, have you been surprised by a special connection to someone (date or friend)? Or do you know a Sheila-Jason story? What lesson does that kind of a story offer you?

—Jen learned that her preference had been based on being unbalanced. Her preferences did not come from health. Consider such possibilities listed on pages 95–96. Where, if at all, do you see yourself in this list? What fears may be determining (or could determine) the people you date?

- "In the shallow areas of preferences—like physical shape, personality types, and others—we suggest you be open to casually dating anyone of good character. Why say no if the person is of safe character?" What is new to you about this perspective on dating? Do you agree or disagree with this approach? Explain.

The warning here is to observe your preferences and value them, but be open to the fact that they may not be so good for you after all. God may know something that you don't know. Be open to getting to know people who are not like you assume you would like, and see what might develop. If a person is not dangerous, go out and have a good time!

Important Preferences (page 96)

On the other hand, some preferences are good to have. You will probably want to have someone who shares common interests, common goals, and common values.

- **Common Interests**—Common interests help you determine how you spend your free time. Most strong relationships include at least some common interests.

—What do you enjoy doing? Think about how you spend your free time and the activities that give you energy and joy.

—Why would sharing some of your interests be good for a dating relationship and someday a marriage?

—Where are you going or could you go to meet people who share your top two or three interests?

- **Common Goals**—Common goals determine how you spend your life. Your goals will affect where you live, what career you choose, how you spend your time and money, and even how you develop your character and walk with God.

—What goals do you have for yourself? To answer that question, you may find it easier to think about where you'd like to be in five years, in ten, and in twenty-five.

—Why is it wise to know what your goals are before getting seriously involved with someone?

—Where are you going or could you go to meet people who are pursuing similar goals?

• **Common Values**—The third area where preferences are important is the area of character. Someone's character is what you are going to experience if you stay in a relationship very long.

—What traits do you value in a person's character? Be as specific as possible.

—When, if ever, have you compromised your standards regarding a person's character? Why did you do that? What might keep you from making that mistake again?

—To search for character that shows the fruit of the Spirit—love, patience, kindness, and so forth (Galatians 5:22–23)—would be a good dating goal. Where might you undertake that search?

Minor Imperfections You Can Live With (page 98)

No one is perfect. Every person you date will be a person who will sin and let you down. However, as you evaluate the people you date, remember a few things.

- First, you can live with sinners who have the ability to see when they have wronged you, to confess it, to care about how they have hurt you, and to work hard not to continue in that pattern.

—Which of these four areas do you need to work on so you can be a sinner folks can live with?

—Review the traits of someone who demonstrates the ability to work on their imperfections (listed on page 99). Why is such a person who meets these criteria a good bet? (Also, which traits do you need to develop?)

- A person of good character will still fail, but generally they have "yellow-light" sins that you can live with—as long as the person sees these problems in him- or herself and deals with them.

—Look at the list of things that will annoy you but won't kill you, things you could learn to accept in mild doses (pages 99–100). Which areas can you work on in yourself?

—What do these items listed suggest to you about where you could grow in being accepting and supportive of a fellow sinner? Put differently, what do you see about your tendency to be judgmental or perfectionistic?

None of us gets everything right in relationships, and as a result we all are somewhat of a pain to be with at times. That is normal. Also, since you have to date sinners, decide which sins you can live with, or at least work with.

Major Imperfections You Can't (and Shouldn't) Live With (page 100)

Not all sins are in the yellow category. Some are bright red—as in stop! Some sins are more damaging than others. As Jesus said clearly, there are "weightier" aspects of God's law, and those are the ones that destroy relationships and hurt people, things like the lack of justice, mercy, and faithfulness (see Matthew 23:23).

- Character begins with yourself. So, in Psalm 101:2–8, David lists things he decided to avoid: faithlessness, perversity, evil, slander, pride, deceit, and wickedness.

—What are you doing to build character in yourself, godly character that is devoid of the traits David listed?

—"The Bible tells us over and over that some people are worthy of trust and some are not (Matthew 7:6). It is not 'unforgiving' to have good boundaries and to not trust a certain kind of person." When would acting on this truth have spared you or someone you know some heartache?

- In our book *Safe People*, we listed some other traits that are destructive to relationships. The lists are reprinted on pages 102–3 of *Boundaries in Dating*.

—***Destructive Personal Traits:*** When have you seen someone hurt (or been hurt yourself) by someone acting out one or more of these traits?

—Which traits listed point out areas where you could be growing?

—**Destructive Interpersonal Traits:** When have you seen someone hurt (or been hurt yourself) by someone acting on one or more of these traits?

—And, again, which traits listed are areas where you could be growing?

- Review the steps to take if you find yourself in a dating relationship with someone who has a pattern of these destructive personal and/or interpersonal traits (page 104). Who in your support system can help you stand strong if and when you need to take these steps?

- The best tests of a relationship are the standards set forth in God's Word and how your own heart feels as you are in a relationship with a person.

—When have you seen a relationship or been involved in one that violated the guidelines in God's Word? What kept the person or you yourself from ending that relationship? How would you handle the relationship differently today?

—When have you seen someone in a relationship with—or when have you yourself been in a relationship with—a person who injured you, left you feeling bad about yourself and love, and hurt you in other ways? Why did you or that person stay in the relationship, tolerating things that you should not have allowed? How would you handle that relationship differently today?

If you are feeling a lot of bad things as a result of being with a person—not simply the pain that comes from having a relationship, but injurious pain—let that be a sign. Protect yourself by knowing what you feel and value, and have the courage to stick to what you value for your dating life. Ultimately, you will get what you value. Value good things, and say no to things that destroy.

Before You Close the Book . . .

- Which take-away tip on pages 105–6 do you most need to take away?

Good and holy God, thank you that you forgive my sins, that you offer repentance and transformation by your Spirit, that you work in me to grow me and to change my destructive ways. May you also be growing in me the wisdom I need to recognize yellow lights and red lights in relationships; the patience I need for living with yellow-light sinners (patience I myself need from them!); and boldness to take a stand and say no to the red-light things I should not tolerate in a relationship. In Jesus' name. Amen.

Chapter 7

Don't Fall in Love with Someone You Wouldn't Be Friends With

Remember Stephanie? She would fall in love with men that she would not choose as friends. There would just be this attraction that she did not have the ability to justify in any rational sense. Friendship, communication, and good times "just hanging out" were always outside the scope of who she was having romantic feelings for.

A Common Problem (page 109)

Many singles we've known share Stephanie's problem. Perhaps you do too.

- When, if ever, have you been attracted to one kind of person but have been better friends with another? Describe the two types. Which of Stephanie's statements could be your own words?

- When, if ever, have you been attracted to someone who was not good for you at all? What about that person was not good for you? And what do you think that attraction was all about?

- Why is "don't fall in love with someone you wouldn't be friends with" good advice?

The Split (page 110)

Perhaps, like the woman who called in to the radio show, you've thought that there were only two kinds of men (or women) in the world: those who are attractive but have no character and those who have good character and spiritual depth but no attractiveness. This woman was blind to her own responsibility. She couldn't see that there was more to the dynamic than some sort of external explanation.

- The problem the woman described is a common and very resolvable one that we see people grow out of all the time.

—Review the six steps we tell singles who have this problem (pages 111–13).

—Which statement(s) in each step did you mentally or perhaps actually highlight?

Step 1:

Step 2:

Step 3:

Step 4:

Step 5:

Step 6:

—What call to personal growth do you hear as you review those highlighted statements? Do you, for instance, need to look at yourself or your dating patterns more honestly? Do you need to rely more on someone in your support system for help with that honesty?

Now let's look at the internal dynamics that lead people to the conclusion that not one attractive person has depth and spiritual qualities and that none who have depth and good character are attractive.

Resolving the Split (page 113)

Safe People, Changes That Heal, and Hiding from Love can help you work through the kinds of issues that cause you to be attracted to the wrong kind of person. The main point here is that you need to have some good boundaries with yourself in terms of allowing yourself to get further into relationships with someone you would not want to be friends with. Here are some reasons that you may be attracted to the wrong kind of person.

- *Unresolved Family-of-Origin Issues*—If you had problems in the family you grew up in, those problems may surface in your dating relationships.

—One woman was attracted to a person like a parent she struggled with. The other was attracted to someone who was the diametrical opposite of the hurtful parent. What, if anything, do their experiences suggest about underlying issues in your own dating history?

—What unresolved family-of-origin issues, if any, might surface in your dating relationships? What could you do to resolve those issues before they interfere?

- *Unintegrated Parts of Yourself*—Another prime reason you may be attracted to people who would not be good for you is that you are looking to resolve some aspect of yourself that you have never faced.

—Often if you do not possess a certain quality, you are drawn to someone who possesses it in the extreme. When, if ever, have you seen this happen or perhaps experienced it for yourself? What character quality and its opposite were involved?

—Sometimes a person is attracted to a bad thing. When, if ever, have you seen or been the "saint" falling head over heals with a "sinner"? If you're thinking of your own experience here, what will you do to find safe relationships to integrate the parts of yourself you are ashamed of so you will be neither "good" nor "bad" in a split way, but *real* with both good and bad parts?

—Sometimes a person has a pain or hurt that she has never faced and is drawn to someone who has a lot of pain and problems. When have you seen or been part of this classic codependent syndrome? Describe the dynamics of that relationship.

—Whatever is in your heart is what you are going to find yourself dealing with, in one way or another, as you date. So what can you do to guard your heart (Proverbs 4:23) and make it healthy so you will not be attracted to the wrong kinds of people?

- ***Defensive Hope***—Have you had a lot of disappointment and loss in your life? If so, it may be difficult for you to let go of things, even things that are not good. You may have developed a pattern of "defensive hope."

—When, if ever, have you hoped for a date to change as a defense against the loss that would come with letting go of the relationship? Describe that experience and what you were thinking and feeling as you chose to stay in the unhealthy relationship.

—What would you say to someone in a similar situation today? What might help that person realize that the grief of letting go would not swallow him up?

- **Romanticizing**—A "hopeless romantic" may be vulnerable to charmers who don't have the underlying character to carry on a lasting relationship. "Charm is deceptive" (Proverbs 31:30), and charmers and their prey are unable to get past romanticizing to real intimacy.

—Do you describe yourself as a "hopeless romantic"? Do you have a long-standing Cinderella complex ("Someday my prince will come")? Or are your fantasies a defense against depression or other kinds of disappointments? What can you do or who can you talk to to get a handle on what your romanticism is all about?

—If you have a tendency to romanticize everything, then you are avoiding the reality of what is going on. And the reality is what you are going to have to live with. That said, what good aspect of being a romantic does a person do well to hang on to?

- **Undeveloped Intimacy**—Some people have not ever been connected with and known at a very deep level. At their most vulnerable parts of their heart, they have never been related to. So, they don't know what real connection and intimacy is.

—When, if ever, have you been connected with or known at a deep level? Why is that—or would that—experience be an advantage as you date?

—Are you aware of your undeveloped ability to be intimate? Does your dating history suggest that your detachment has been drawn to detachment? If you answer yes to either of these questions, what step toward a cure will you make? Specifically, what healing relationships—that are not romantic in nature—will you invest in so that all of your parts can be related to and find connection?

Friendship Is the Path (page 118)

Romance is great. Sexuality is great. Attraction is great. But here is the key: *If all of those are not built upon lasting friendship and respect for the person's character, something is wrong.*

- Think about lasting relationships you know of. What evidence do you see that each is built on friendship first? You might even talk to one of the parties involved.

- The best boundary that you can have in your dating life is to begin every relationship with an eye toward friendship.

—What does this advice mean in terms of what you do with a person in the early stages of a relationship? Put differently, what kinds of activities would help you see whether that person could be a friend?

—Why should you not believe your feelings in the early stages of a possible dating relationship?

You want your best friends to be honest, faithful, deep, spiritual, responsible, connecting, growing, loving, and the like. Make sure that those qualities are also present in the person you are falling in love with.

Before You Close the Book . . .

- Which take-away tip on pages 119–120 do you most need to take away?

Lord God, the advice sounds simple enough, but that doesn't mean it's easy to live out. "Don't fall in love with someone you wouldn't be friends with." Please help me to be honest about my relationships— honest before you, honest with myself, and honest with a close friend or two—so that I can avoid some of the heartache that dating can bring. Also, as actual dating experiences or stories in this book show me where I can be growing, please help that growth happen. And teach me to value friendship—a friendship rooted in you—as the underlying foundation of any romantic relationship. In Jesus' name. Amen.

Chapter 8

Don't Ruin a Friendship Out of Loneliness

*R*emember Ted and Ellen? Their friendship is an example of two things. First, it illustrates how much good can come from healthy opposite-sex relationships. And second, it shows how much grief they spared themselves by not pursuing a romantic relationship when the feelings were simply not there.

- Are you blessed by a healthy and platonic opposite-sex relationship? What good has come out of that for you?

- When, if ever, have you tried—or seen someone else try—to date a friend? What happened to the friendship?

The topic of this chapter is to help you experience the good that comes from friendships and avoid the problems that come from making friendships into something they are not.

Romanticizing a Friendship (page 122)

Romantic feelings come from an idealization of the other person. When that idealization is caused by neediness being romanticized, a perfectly good friendship can be ruined.

- Romanticization occurs when a lonely person is unable to safely feel and act appropriately upon his lonely emotions.

71

—When do you feel lonely—and what do you do in response to those feelings?

—One type of loneliness indicates that we need to be in day-to-day contact with others. Another type, however, is a chronic, long-standing sense of emptiness in life, no matter what the circumstances. Do you struggle with the second? If so, know that it's an indication that something is broken in your soul and needs to be repaired in God's healing process. What will you do to take a step toward that healing?

Whatever type of loneliness people experience, there are several causes of romanticization.

- **Conflicts in Experiencing Dependency**—People who romanticize often are unable to feel their dependency for what it is: dependency.

—Are you unable to feel your dependency as dependency? If so, which, if any, of the five reasons listed on page 124 may be behind that inability?

—How have you dealt with loneliness in the past? Have you gotten plugged into a healthy relationship—or have you instead felt irritation, depression, addictive drives, and romantic cravings?

—If you're feeling lonely right now, do you see it as a good or a bad thing? Why—and what will you do to deal with that loneliness?

- **Failures in Relating to the Same Sex**—Often, those who romanticize their friends have a history of not being able to safely and deeply connect to the same sex so they keep trying to have significant connection with members of the opposite sex.

—Where, if at all, do you see yourself limited in your ability to connect with members of the same sex? See the bulleted items listed on page 125. What will you do about any truth you realize about yourself here?

—The needs that romanticizers have are pre-adult needs, such as belonging, being safe, and feeling comforted and loved. What can you do to let God meet these needs? What safe nonromantic relationships can also help meet these needs?

- **Idealizing Romance**—Some people think that romance is the highest form of friendship. Many people who are "into" romance (watch out!) feel that friendship is a grade lower than a romance. Don't get caught in the idea that you are missing out by keeping your friend as "only" your friend.

—Romantic relationships are not better than friendships. They are different and meet different needs. List some of the differences and some of the different needs that are met.

—When, if ever, have you thought that romantic relationship is better than a friendship and tried to elevate the friendship? What happened to the friendship—and what did you learn from the experience?

- **Rescue/Caretaking Roles**—Sometimes, people who get caught up in romanticizing have tendencies to get into certain ways of relating called *rescuing* and *caretaking*. The "rescuee" will signal a need for someone to take care of him. The "caretaker" will receive the signal and go support, comfort, or solve the problems of the rescuee.

—When, if ever, have you fallen first into this pattern and then fallen in love with either your caretaker or the one you cared for?

—Why is this an unhealthy dynamic in a dating relationship?

- **Impulsiveness**—Some people struggle with romanticization because they have difficulty with their drives and impulses. They become sexually intimate (an oxymoron) very quickly, or are into quick, intense, "deep" connections.

—When, if ever, have you or someone you know tried to take either of these shortcuts to a significant relationship? What happened?

—Why doesn't impulsive romanticization lead to satisfying relationships?

How Can I Know If This Is a Friendship or a Romance? (page 128)

How can you tell if your present relationship is the real thing? Here are some ways to see if you are wrecking a friendship by romanticizing.

- ***Get Connected Outside of the Relationship***—We all need people who will love us, support us, and tell us the truth on a continual basis.

—Who can tell you the truth about yourself—and that includes the truth about your dating relationships?

—If you aren't connected to others, you'll be navigating the waters of dating (and life!) alone, and that's not wise. Where will you start looking for some safe places where you can relate without a date?

- ***Evaluate the Fruits of the Relationship***—What do you value in the relationship? True romance and romanticization are after very different goals.

—What does the chart on page 129 help you recognize about healthy romance vs. romanticized friendship?

—What does the chart help you realize about any past or current relationship?

—How can the information in the chart help you in a current relationship or prepare you to be wise in a future one?

- *Get Feedback*—Turn to one of your truth-telling friends for some input.

—Ask your friends if you are a romance addict. Also ask them to evaluate what kind of friend you are to them. Find out if they know the deeper parts of who you are.

—Then act on what you learn from your friends. What about their feedback surprised you? Where do you see an opportunity for personal growth?

If You Are on the Receiving End . . . (page 130)

Maybe you, like Natalie, have been or are in a relationship that would be better off as a friendship.

- What can you learn from Natalie and Spencer's relationship? Consider why each continued in it.

- Did you identify with Natalie's experience? If so, how are you part of the problem with the relationship? What is a better way for you to deal with the issues that are keeping you in the relationship?

You do yourself and your date no favors by avoiding the reality. Pay attention to things like openness, freedom, mutuality, and the like. If you avoid the issues, you can keep a lonely person from ever dealing with a problem that God wants to help him with, and you can waste a lot of your time and energy. Be part of the solution for both of you.

Before You Close the Book . . .

• Which take-away tip on pages 131–32 do you most need to take away?

Creator God, thank you that you have made me to be in relationship and that you make me feel lonely so I will seek relationship. Help me first and always to seek connectedness with you. Teach me also to build and maintain safe, healthy friendships. Then, when it's time for romance, may I include you and my friends in the process so that the result is healthy romance, not romanticized friendship. In Jesus' name. Amen.

Chapter 9

Beware When Opposites Attract

*C*ompletion. *At our deepest part, we all want and need it. There is within us a God-given desire to find the missing pieces that will finish us. This desire drives us toward relationships. Yet this desire can also be confused with the desires of dating and mating, and bad things can happen. This is the problem of the "opposites attract" mentality.*

Differing Gifts Are Good for Relationships (page 134)

Indeed, there is a lot of value in people bringing strengths to a relationship. Our lives are always enriched by being connected to others who have abilities we don't have.

- When have you seen the value of complementary gifts in the business world? In the church? Be specific on both counts.

- When have you grown because, in humility, you asked for what you didn't possess?

We are enriched and helped by taking advantage of the differing gifts of others.

The Problem of Opposite Attractions (page 135)

We should use and appreciate the abilities of those who have what we don't. However, the danger occurs when we make opposing styles or abilities a basis for relationship.

- More of a lover than a fighter, Lindsey was attracted by Alex, who was strong, confident, and had no problems entering into conflict for what he believed was right.

—What danger to her own personal growth did that relationship hold for Lindsey?

—What did you learn from the way both Alex and Lindsey dealt with their differences?

- The Lindsey-Alex situation could have ended in a variety of ways (listed on pages 136–37). When have you seen or been involved in an opposites-attract relationship that didn't work out well? Describe what happened and what could have been done differently for a happier ending.

Opposite-driven relationships often confuse dependency with true love. Dependency is only part of love. It is not the full expression of love. The full expression of love is to give back from a full heart.

Why Opposites Attract (page 137)

What is it about opposites that people find so attractive? Why are we attracted to our opposite? There are several answers to this question.

- ***We Do Not Want to Work at Developing Ourselves***—The essence of the opposite issue is not really about the other person. It is about using another person to avoid dealing with our own souls.

—When have you or someone you know piggybacked on another person's strengths instead of addressing an area of growth that needed work?

—Why is this an unhealthy motive for dating?

- **We Want to Be Complete**—We are drawn to those who possess what we do not, so that we can internalize and own that trait for ourselves.

—When has a mentor, teacher, counselor, or friend helped you develop a character trait? Be specific about the process and how you benefited.

—Why is dating not a good arena in which to develop oneself in a specific and important aspect of growth?

- **We Are Afraid of Dealing with Our Deficits**—Another reason that opposites attract is our fear of looking at our own character flaws. Self-exploration and change can be scary.

—What fears (some of which are listed on page 139) have been or are issues for you? How, if at all, have those fears played themselves out in your dating life?

—What experiences or lessons from the family you grew up in underlie the fear you just identified?

—What role can a support group or a safe friend play in helping you deal with your fear?

- **We Are Spiritually Lazy**—It is simply easier to have others do for us what we don't want to do for ourselves. This is the nature of immaturity, or "spiritual laziness."

—Remember the examples of immaturity (page 140), of people failing to take ownership for what they have internalized and continuing to demand that others provide it? Which scenario, if any, have you seen or lived out yourself?

—Did those descriptions on page 140 suggest to you areas where you might be spiritually lazy? Explain.

—Whether the problem be fear or laziness, we need to deal with our own deficits instead of looking to a date to heal them. What role could a support group or a safe friend play in helping you with your laziness and irresponsibility?

- **We Rely on Our Partner's Gifts Rather Than Dealing with Our Character Deficits**—Sometimes the problem can be a confusion between giftedness and character deficits.

—Do you find yourself continually needing to go to your date for things you should be doing for yourself—or do you see that pattern in your past? What are or were those "things"?

—Three gauges of health are listed on pages 140–41. What invitations to personal growth do you find in these statements?

What Happens When Oppositeness Rules (page 141)

Though opposites do attract, they can have their dangers as well. Kim and Pete are a good example of the kinds of problems that occur when oppositeness rules.

- **Loss of Freedom**—Why does loss of freedom happen when oppositeness rules?

- **Resentment**—Why is resentment to be expected when oppositeness rules?

- **Confusion in Responsibilities**—Kim stopped taking responsibility for her friendships, and Pete stopped taking responsibility for how he conducted his relationship with Kim. Why does such failure to take full ownership of one's life result when oppositeness rules?

- **Parent-Child Struggles**—Explain how a dating relationship between opposites can take on some parent-child dynamics.

What have you learned from Kim and Pete? What new understanding about relational dynamics and/or what insight about yourself have you gained that will help you in a dating relationship?

Dependency and Growth (page 143)

Dependency on the love and support of others is a good thing (Ecclesiastes 4:10), but dependency has an ultimate purpose: growth. We are to take in the love, comfort, and instruction of others in order to grow spiritually and emotionally.

- Dependency that does not lead to growth ultimately creates more immaturity in the person. When have you seen dependency serve immaturity, not growth, or perhaps even experienced that kind of regression for yourself?

- What can you learn from Hugh and Sandy's relationship? What new understanding about relational dynamics and/or what insight about yourself have you gained that will help you in a dating relationship?

Opposites and Maturity (page 145)

In our experience, the degree of attraction that opposites have for each other is often diagnostic of the couple's maturity. Attraction based on values is much more mature than attraction based on what you don't have inside.

- In mature couples, opposite traits are simply not a major issue. The two are not drawn to opposite traits due to their own deficits. They are drawn to values that they share. Who in your life illustrates this maturity? You might want to talk to these people about how they're alike, how they're different, and how the differences make the relationship fulfilling, rich, and satisfying.

- Many immature people are ultimately looking for a parent to take care of part of them that they aren't taking care of in themselves. Where have you seen this principle acted out in real life—or when, if ever, have you fallen into this pattern? Why does this make for relational struggles?

Make oppositeness a nonissue. Look more for character, love, and values than "who has what." Fall for someone who calls you into love, growth, and God. And then appreciate that person's unique differences.

Before You Close the Book ...

- Which take-away tip on pages 146–147 do you most need to take away?

> *Creator God, you've made us human beings complex creatures with different gifts and strengths, and you call us to develop those areas of our character where we are weak. Help me recognize my character deficits and then look to you rather than to a date as I get involved in the growth process. And when it's time to date, help me be an agent of growth, healing, and change for my date even as I encourage him/her to play that role in my life. In Jesus' name. Amen.*

Part Three

SOLVING DATING PROBLEMS: WHEN YOU'RE PART OF THE PROBLEM

Chapter 10

Adapt Now, Pay Later

*I*t's better to find out in the early months of a relationship that you are with someone who cannot adapt to your wishes than to find out much later.

- When, if ever, have you done more than the normal initial adapting in order not to jeopardize a developing relationship? When—and how—did you realize that things went smoothly only as long as you adapted to your date and that your date was unable to deal with your needs and desires?

Keri had learned a lesson that you may have learned the hard way, too: don't be someone you are not just to gain someone's love. If you do, the person that your loved one is loving is not you. It is the role that you are playing and not your true self who is being loved.

Wishes, Needs, and Desires (page 154)

As Keri discovered, you cannot act forever. You are a person, and you cannot go through life without pursuing your own wishes, needs, and desires—nor should you.

- What warning and wisdom can you take from our marriage counseling experiences?

- Explain how healthy boundaries can keep you from adapting too much or, put differently, can help you be honest about your wishes, needs, and desires.

- The lesson of this chapter is to *be yourself from the beginning*, and then you can find someone who is authentic as well.

—What, if anything, keeps you from being yourself? What fears, past hurts, or daunting risks prompt you to be more compliant than may be healthy and wise?

—Keri's friend Sandy helped her see reality and cope with the loss of Steve. What safe friend is close enough to see the dynamics of your dating relationship and whether you are really being yourself?

A relationship between two authentic people has mutuality and partnership. It has give and take. It has equality. It has sharing and mutual self-sacrifice for the sake of the other and the relationship. If you are a real person from the start, a relationship of mutuality has a chance of developing.

Bad Attractions (page 156)

People who are selfish and controlling can only be that way if they are in relationship with someone who is adaptive. If someone stands up to them and is honest about his or her wants and desires, then the controlling person has to learn to share or gets frustrated and goes away.

- Again, if you tend to be adaptive, what is fueling that tendency and what can you do to heal the underlying hurt or meet the hidden need in a healthier way?

- Similarly, what may be keeping you from being honest about wants and desires? And, again, what can you do to heal the underlying hurt or meet the hidden need in a healthier way?

Being honest and straightforward about simple things can help you find out quickly if you are dating someone who is able to share, or someone who has to have his or her way all the time. This knowledge will be helpful now and essential for the future.

Before You Close the Book . . .

- Which take-away tip on page 157 do you most need to take away?

*Holy God, I've seen it before in this book, and I've seen it again
just now: the importance of being truthful about who I am, about what
I want and desire. As I take the risk of having someone know me, give
me the courage to be me. And help me live in the light of truth in
small ways as well as big ways. In Jesus' name. Amen.*

Chapter 11

Too Much, Too Fast

*T*he problem of premature commitment and overinvolvement in a dating relationship is
a common one. Whether the relationship leads to marriage or a break up, the couple is
typified by a drivenness to become highly committed, a process that takes less than a normal amount of time (Ecclesiastes 3:1).

- When have you seen, or been involved in, a too-much, too-fast relationship?

- "Frontloading" a relationship means becoming deeply committed very soon in the
  game rather than going through a process of gradually becoming closer over time.
  What are some advantages of a gradual process?

- Why do we suggest that a dating relationship last for at least a year, not including
  engagement?

*In a too-much, too-fast situation, the couple sees time as the adversary, and actively
resists any more of it than is necessary.*

Why Wait? (page 160)

Why should you wait, take time, and gradually become closer to a person to whom you are enormously attracted? We'll look at three answers to that question.

- ***Relationships Do Not Tolerate Shortcuts***—First we have to understand the nature of relationships as God designed them. Relationships grow in a healthy manner only as they undergo experiences, and there is no shortcut to experiences.

    —When have you been surprised by who a person (friend, business associate, or date) really was once you got to know that person through shared experiences? Comment on what the shared experiences revealed that you hadn't known about that person before.

    —Review the list of eight time-consuming dating activities listed on page 161. What is the value of each? Put differently, why aren't shortcuts possible?

When people meet and marry quickly, their success is due more to their own character than to going through the process the right way. There is no microwave dating that makes any sense. Go through the seasons of life with the person you believe might be the right one for you, the person in whom you see a healthy potential for marriage.

- ***A Measure of Importance***—Second, the time involved in dating someone should reflect the significance of the relationship. Simply put, the more important a decision is, the more time it should take to make it. Our most important human relationship should warrant the time due it.

    —Review the aspects of marriage listed on page 163. Which of those serve as a wake-up call to the seriousness of marriage?

—When, if ever, have you experienced loneliness within a relationship? How did that compare to being alone?

A bad marriage is probably more painful than a bad single state. Living alone within the marriage contract makes the disconnection feelings so acute that many people leave the marriage. With such serious factors at stake, it is worth it to take ample time to get to know someone.

- **The Nature of Love**—Another reason to take your time is that this is a necessary part of learning how to love. Dating should not only produce a mate. It should also develop within you the ability to love that mate deeply and well. And love, as the Bible defines it, is a stance of working for the best for another person.

—When has a friendship or dating relationship taught you something about how to love? Explain.

—Taking time in your dating relationship helps you clarify the distinction between need and love. What relationship that you've seen or perhaps been involved in seemed propelled forward by the kind of needs listed on page 164? Describe what happened.

Reasons for speeding up the pace of a relationship involve some sort of dependency and may put you in a child or parent role at some level. And one of the worst things you can do is try to reparent someone you are dating. It usually causes confusion and pain for both parties.

Am I Going Too Fast? (page 165)

It can be difficult to tell if you are going too fast. Love does have an individual pace for people. Some can safely progress more quickly than others. Also there is such a thing as going too slowly.

- When have you seen someone going too fast in a relationship? What happened? As a friend, what did you do or would you have liked to have done?

- Review the four ways of determining if you yourself might commit too quickly. What lesson do those four indicators offer you?

As a rule of thumb, it is better to err on the side of caution.

Why We Don't Wait (page 165)

If there are such benefits to dating at a gradual pace, then why do we see so much over-involvement? Here are some main reasons people dive into the shallow end of love.

- ***Loneliness***—Loneliness is one of the most painful yet necessary experiences in life.

   —Why is loneliness a necessary experience? What good comes from feeling lonely? Speak, if you can, from personal experience.

   —Why is dating not the kind of relationship that cures loneliness? You might be able to speak from personal experience here, too.

- ***Difficulty in Leaving Home***—Sometimes two people seem to "couple" very quickly because they have not finished the task of emotionally leaving home. They are unable to navigate single life and opt more for the marriage state than for the person.

—What did you learn (or do you hope to learn) about how to live life on your own during your college years and early twenties? Be specific about the "relating" areas of life as well as the "doing" areas.

—What, if anything, do your feelings about being single tell you about whether or not you have finished leaving home emotionally? What dependencies, if any, are you still working through?

- **Difficulties in Sustaining Friendships**—Some people will overcommit due to problems in making deep, sustaining friendships. They struggle with what are called attachment issues.

  —Do you have difficulty sustaining friendships? Do you have a hard time getting truly close to people? Do you find it hard to trust others? Do you feel relief when you are alone? Could a yes answer be an indication of attachment issues? If so, what will you do to start resolving them?

  —What can you learn from the experience of my artist friend and his wife (page 168)?

- **Perfectionism**—Some perfectionists become quickly committed to a person who seems to represent every weakness they don't have. In this way she is still in relationship with all of the parts of herself, yet she doesn't have to take ownership of them.

—What is not worked on in our souls is often found in those we choose. When have you seen an "angel" woman quickly commit to a "devilish" guy? What traits did the angel not have to take ownership of in that situation?

—There's another way to deal with perfectionism. Do you know (or are you yourself) a perfectionist who delays commitment in quest of the perfect partner? Why is this effort futile? What would be a better focus for the perfectionist? Hint: it has to do with personal growth.

What Should I Do? (page 169)

If your dating life tends to be too much, too fast, there are several things you can do about it. The steps are not enjoyable, and they involve some work. But if you are tired of the roller coaster of intense but failed relationships, the effort is worth it.

• Review the steps listed below and defined on pages 169–70. Below, note the truths that you especially need to hear and/or the specific things you need to do.

—Identify What Is Driving the Pace:

—Get a Life:

—Deliberately Slow the Pace to Diagnose the Relationship:

—Investigate Who Is Contributing to the Pace:

—Ask Friends for Feedback:

Before You Close the Book . . .

- Which take-away tip on pages 170–71 do you most need to take away?

Lord God, I'm not good at waiting, and waiting can be even harder in the dating arena. Help me to trust in your good plans for me enough that I will move slowly in my relationships, taking time to seek your will, to hear the counsel of friends, to work on the issues I need to work on, and to learn to love as you would have me love. Then, Lord, when the time is right, make me patient with the process of love and able to experience and enjoy its growth day by day. In Jesus' name. Amen.

Chapter 12

Don't Get Kidnapped

Nick was nice, but he was kidnapping Debbie. She was being separated from her friends, support systems, and everything that was important to her, even her values.

- Reread the story of Nick and Debbie. Where, if at all, do you see yourself in this scenario?

- What warning does Debbie's experience offer you? Consider, for instance, why she didn't notice that she was being kidnapped.

- What do you appreciate about Debbie's friends? Who in your life might do for you what Debbie's friends did for her?

After her two wake-up calls, Debbie got reconnected to her friends and then stayed connected. Her friends gave her several important ingredients that every dating relationship must have in order to be based in reality. Let's look at those ingredients.

A Feedback Base to See Reality (page 178)

Being "in love," in the beginning of a relationship, is an illness. The illness is the inability to see reality. For the very state of "being in love" is a state of idealization, where the other person is not really viewed through the eyes of reality.

- What chunks of reality about a person you've been in love with have you not seen? What helped you finally see them? More specifically, what role did friends play—or, to do some Monday-morning quarterbacking, would you have liked them to play?

- When, if ever, have you had the opportunity to offer a reality-based perspective of a friend's date? What did you do and how was your input received? If that opportunity comes again, what will you do?

When we fall in love, we can't see the idealization we're doing or the fact that we're becoming someone other than who we really are. But hopefully our friends can.

A Support Base to Deal with Reality (page 179)

We do not deal with reality either because we do not see it or we see it and are unable or unwilling to deal with it. Many times we know that there is something wrong, but we cannot find it in ourselves to break away or do the right thing.

- When have you relied on friends to help you through some of life's hard times, perhaps even the end of a dating relationship?

- What did your friends offer you? See Ecclesiastes 4:9–12 and the list on page 180.

Some dating relationships need to end and the time has come (Ecclesiastes 3:6), but the person is not strong enough to do what is needed. Friends and community can be a lifesaver in that situation.

Connection to All the Parts of Her (page 181)

As Debbie was dating Nick, she was losing parts of herself. That is not what happens in a good relationship. A good relationship helps us to become more of who God made us to be, not less.

- When, if ever, have you lost parts of yourself in a dating relationship or perhaps even in a friendship? What parts did you lose?

- When have you noticed a friend's personality change—for better or worse—in a dating relationship? Be specific about the changes and what you did, if anything, if the change was for the worse. When have you later realized that you yourself experienced a personality change in a dating relationship? What were those changes—and how will you keep from falling into that trap again?

If you are continuing to "do life" as you were before you started dating, you remain yourself, and the two of you get to know all of who each other is. Friends help you stay connected to the things you were connected with before you started dating.

Grounding in Spiritual Values That Make Life Work (page 182)

Our values are the architecture of life. They shape the way our life is going to be. When we begin to let our values slip, our life takes a direction that does not have a good end.

- What values form the architecture of your life? List eight or ten.

- In what ways might a dating relationship tempt you to compromise on these values? Thinking about this in advance may help you avoid some heartache.

Our community is one of the delivery systems that God has designed to help us stay grounded in our values and in him. Debbie's friends confronted the ways that she was getting off the path of what was good for her. And they did it like God does, with her best interests in mind.

Separateness and Development Apart from the Relationship (page 183)

A relationship that gets rid of one's individual life and friends, time, and space, is not a healthy relationship.

- When have you seen a relationship rob a person of friends, time, and space the way Nick robbed Debbie? What helpful difference would friends have made in that situation?

- When, if ever, have you gotten rid of your space and individuality and basically fused with a person in a dating relationship? Looking back, explain as best you can why that happened. Be sure to address what had happened (or what you had let happen!) to your friends.

Your friends are an important space-giving freedom that will help you to be healthier and more well-rounded. In addition, they will notice if you are losing them to a dating relationship.

Safe Dating (page 184)

One aspect of safe dating is to remain connected to your friends and support system. Make sure that you are not vulnerable to what you cannot see, and let other people help you see clearly. Stay connected, stay safe, and stay wise.

• Which of the following, if any, might you be at risk for?

—Getting kidnapped by controlling or dependent people

—Getting kidnapped by your own wishes to be close to someone

—Giving up all important things because of your lack of boundaries

—Living in a vacuum; lacking a community

• What specific step will you take to prevent the risk(s) you just flagged?

• If you have a strong support system in place, how will you let them be involved in your current or your next dating relationship? Be specific—and remember this plan and act on it when the time comes.

Before You Close the Book . . .

- Which take-away tip on pages 185–86 do you most need to take away?

Lord God, you designed me to be in relationship with you and you call us, your children, into community with one another. Thank you that, because of that, I don't ever need to enter a dating relationship alone— and help me not to! Then, once a relationship begins, Lord, help me stay in touch with my friends. After all, "wounds from a friend can be trusted" (Proverbs 27:6). So help me hear your voice through what my friends have to say about things I cannot see. And help me always to heed your will and live every aspect of my life, including my dating, your way. In Jesus' name. Amen.

Chapter 13

Kiss False Hope Good-bye

*H*ope is one of the greatest virtues (1 Corinthians 13:13). The kind of hope God wants us to have is the kind that "does not disappoint" (Romans 5:5), the kind that is based on the love that God has for us. But the Bible speaks of another kind of hope as well. It is the hope that "makes the heart sick" (Proverbs 13:12), hope that is never realized, hope that does not give life.

- What kind of hope had Robbie engaged in for five years before he came to see me (Dr. Cloud)?

- When, if ever, have you—like Robbie—engaged in hope that was denial and wishful thinking? What helped you finally realize you had no basis for your hope?

Without hope, we give up and give in to all sorts of evil. We need hope to persevere. But when we hope and hope and nothing happens and there is no reason to keep hoping, then despair settles in. So what is the role of hope in dating?

Good Hope and Bad Hope in Your Dating Life (page 189)

Since most of you who pick up this book are probably dating, you are looking at the question of when to have hope that the person you are with is going to change. How should hope operate in that scenario? To review, hope should be based in reality.

- To determine whether your hope is merited, consider these two truths.

1. The definition of crazy is to continue to do the same thing expecting different results.

2. The best predictor of the future, without some intervening variable, is the past.

What, if anything, do these two truths suggest to you about whether your current hope is merited? Be honest with yourself.

Chances are that some of you are struggling with whether or not you should give up hope on a certain relationship or continue in it. So let's apply these two truths to some common scenarios.

- ***The person you love treats you in a way that you cannot live with.***

—Review the two paths outlined on pages 190–92. When, if ever, have you walked the first path? What was challenging and what was rewarding about the journey?

—Perhaps the promised change didn't happen despite a good start on the first path. Describe your journey on the second path, if you took it. What change, if any, did you work on in yourself? In what ways, if any, did the relationship improve? What was challenging and what was rewarding about this journey?

—If the person you love treats you in a way that you cannot live with, at what point are you in the process of dealing with it? Are you on the first or second journey? Is it time for a confrontation or some consequences (page 192)? Is it time to try the two tests and see if your hope is merited? With the support of your friends, take the step you need to take.

Is there reason for you to be hoping? Try the two tests! Is there some intervening variable that would make the future different than the past? Or is the person ready to start along the path of change? If that journey happens, there is reason for hope. If not, then you have your answer. It is hopeless.

- To successfully navigate the path of change takes more than love or friendly nagging reminders. Here is what God does to start us on the pathway to growth and give us hope for real change. At each point note what you can learn from God's example about how to deal with your date's change or its absence.

  —*God starts from a loved position:*
  —*God acts righteously:*
  —*God uses others to help:*
  —*God accepts reality about the person, grieves his expectations, and forgives:*
  —*God gives change a chance:*
  —*God is longsuffering:*
  —*God separates:*

- ***A person you are dating says that he or she "likes you" or "loves you" but is not "in love with you," and wants more time to see where the relationship is going.***

—When has a friend of yours been in this situation? What advice did you offer or would you have offered if you'd had the chance?

If this is your current situation, have you tried to take the relationship to a different level from the "just friends" status? What did you do, and how were your efforts received?

—If you have let your feelings be known, but nothing seems to have changed, you could do one of the following:

End the dating relationship.
End the relationship and don't go back for any reason.
Tell him that you are willing to continue if he feels like more time is going to help.
If you are giving the person certain goodies that belong to some sort of commitment more than casual dating, then stop.
Continue with your eyes wide open.

Read the descriptions of each course of action (pages 195–96) and then make your choice. Briefly explain your choice here.

Boundaries have to do with your taking responsibility for reality. You know where the other person stands, and now it is your choice: You can take control of yourself and do what you think is best. If he or she has been acting like more than friends, and then tells you that you are just friends, our advice is to get moving.

- ***Your dating partner won't commit to the relationship's future.***

—If you are currently facing this situation, why might your partner be reluctant? Is he certain about you but doubtful about the timing? Or is he dealing with commitment phobia or commitment allergy? Support your answer with specifics—and get a friend's perspective, too.

—Is the handwriting on the wall? Is it time to pull the plug? What will you do to let your support system do its job for you?

Time does run out, and there is no reason to hope that more time is going to solve anything. Set a limit and stick to it. Give up hope and move on with your life.

- ***You want a friend to like you in a different way, but it is not happening***.

—When, if ever, have you seen friends shift gears and successfully date each other? What prompted the change? In terms of our two-question test, what "intervening variable" may have prompted the change? (See the discussion on page 199.)

—If you currently find yourself in this situation, what statement or action might be an "intervening variable" that sparks a change? (Again, you'll find some options on pages 199–200.)

Just hoping that a person's feelings are going to change for no good reason other than you want them to might be foolish.

Keep Hope Pure (page 200)

To summarize, hope is a virtue; hope should be based on reality; and hope can be distorted and lead to a broken heart. We want you to have hope for your dating life—hope that is based on God, the realities of who you are dating, and the truth of God's principles.

- If you're currently dating, take a look in the mirror which this section offers. Do you have reason for hope in dating? Support your answer with specifics from this passage and from your own life.

- Be specific as you consider what you are doing—or, when you do start dating, what you could do—to . . .

—Be rooted in reality:

—Hope in God:

—Hope in his principles of honesty, communication, vulnerability, humility, love, responsibility, and the like:

—Hope in people of trustworthy character:

—Hope in your own growth:

Hope in God, hope in his principles, hope in people of trustworthy character, and hope in your own growth. Those are truly good reasons for hope. But don't throw hope away on things which have no reality behind them. That kind of hope makes the heart sick.

Before You Close the Book . . .

- Which take-away tip on pages 201–2 do you most need to take away?

*Lord God, thank you for the gift of hope and the truths about hope
I found in this chapter. Make me a person, Lord, who hopes in you, who
stands on your sound principles of growth, and who keeps working with
you on my own growth. And, Lord, keep me rooted in reality and
trusting you even as I turn to you for guidance as to whether or not
I should have hope about a relationship. In Jesus' name. Amen.*

Chapter 14

Boundaries on Blame

If you have a habit of saying to your date things like "Why do you always . . . ," "This is your fault," and "You're so . . . ," these statements may be true, but you may be making things worse. Let's look at setting boundaries on our tendency to blame in dating.

An Honest Legacy (page 203)

We are a species of blamers. Our parents, Adam and Eve, modeled and passed the trait down through the generations (Genesis 3:12–13). What is blaming? It is ascribing responsibility to someone for a fault.

- Explain blame's good function and, if you can, give a personal example of its helpfulness.

- The blame that kills a good dating relationship is when one person sees herself as blameless and attributes almost all of the problems in the relationship to the other person.

—When, if ever, have you been accused of being the source of almost all of the problems in a relationship? In that situation, what did your friend or date not want to realize about himself?

—When, if ever, has denial of your badness or reluctance to confront the reality of your mistakes led you to blame another person for something?

• Blame is one of the gravest problems we face, spiritually and emotionally. It keeps us more concerned about being "good" than about being honest.

—Why should Christians be the least blaming people in the world?

—Why do you—if you do—struggle to accept responsibility for your badness? What freedom from that struggle does Romans 8:1–2 offer you?

The best thing you can do for yourself spiritually as well as in your dating life is to begin learning to accept blame for what is truly your fault, and give up blaming for what is another's fault. Below, we will deal with the negative ways that "bad blaming" can affect your dating life.

Blame: An Obstacle to Intimacy (page 205)

Blaming has the power to negate the growth of intimacy in a dating relationship. When someone feels continually blamed by his date, he is in conflict between his desire to open up and his impulse to withdraw protectively.

- When, if ever, have you experienced this conflict in a dating relationship or a friendship? Or when, if ever, has your blaming put a friend or date into this kind of conflict?

- What lesson about blame does Travis and Morgan's experience offer you? Consider, for instance, who worked on changing.

A State of Mind (page 206)

There is even worse news about blame and dating: You don't even have to verbally blame the other person to ruin the relationship. Blaming can be done inside, in your attitude, without your speaking a word.

- When, if ever, have you felt blamed even though words went unspoken? How was that blame communicated?

- When, if ever, have you wordlessly but clearly blamed a person with silence, coldness, distance, and/or sarcasm? Why did you choose to be indirect?

- Why does blame—unspoken and therefore unaddressed and unresolved—affect how you approach a friend or a date? What are some of those effects?

If you are to deal with blame, deal with it as a problem of the heart as well as the tongue.

How It Works (page 207)

How does blame operate inside the one receiving it? Basically, it is experienced as truth without love, and that always feels like judgment or condemnation.

- When, if ever, has someone spoken truth in love to you? Explain your reaction and how the love helped you deal with the truth.

- Think of a recent confrontation or opportunity for one. How did you balance the truth you wanted to express with love—or how would you have liked to?

The only way to hear truth is in an atmosphere of love (Ephesians 4:15); otherwise, the "blamee" is placed in a state of condemnation that he must fight either by lashing out at you or at himself.

Dating: A Petri Dish for Blame (page 208)

By its very nature, dating is a rich source of blame. People find themselves pointing the finger at the same person who, a few months ago, was their ideal soul mate. There are several reasons for this.

- ***The Exploratory Nature of Dating***—When you do not have to live with someone's faults (you can leave a dating relationship), you are less prone to do the hard work of seeing your part in triggering them.

—If you've been the "blamee," what issues did you see in the person who blamed? How was he/she contributing to the problem you were being blamed for?

—Now think about a friendship or dating relationship that you exited. What prompted your exit? What growth could those issues have prompted in you if you had looked hard enough to see how you were contributing to the problem?

• ***Blaming as a Character Trait***—We all blame to some extent. However, some people have more of a tendency to blame than others.

—What evidence, if any, do you see in your interactions with others, past and present, that blame is one of your character weaknesses? If you're not sure, check in with a close friend and get another perspective.

—The tasks at the end of the chapter will help you work on this character flaw. Before we get there, recruit that friend to hold you accountable to the growth process you'll be undertaking.

• ***The Romantic Intensity of Dating***—The strength of romance can tap into old needs and desires from when we were children. Romantic fires can unearth early parts of a soul that never grew up, and blame can take hold.

—When, if ever, have you had a "Why is he so mad at me?" experience with a date or a friend? What specific growing-up task did the blamer need to do?

—When, if ever, have you been enraged and blamed a date or a friend, greatly overreacting to the offense? What early hurts were fueling your reaction? What are you doing (or what are you going to do) to find healing?

• If you're a blamer, which of the three reasons above may be the greatest factor contributing to your behavior?

The Results of Blame (page 210)

Ultimately, blame is its own and only reward. There is a very sick satisfaction that comes in pointing the finger of judgment at another.

• Blaming provides us with the delusion that we are better than we are and that our biggest problems in life are the sins of other people. How does this wrong perspective on ourselves block our relationship with God and with other people?

• Review the list of some things that can happen in a dating relationship typified by blame (pages 210–11). What does this list suggest about what blaming can do to a relationship?

Dating and Moral Superiority (page 211)

Another way that blame can kill a dating relationship is that the injured person can take on an attitude of moral superiority to her offender.

- When, if ever, has a blamer put himself in a morally superior position to you? What impact did that attitude have on the friendship or dating relationship? You can figure out the answer even if you've never experienced it.

- When, if ever, have you adopted a morally superior attitude toward a friend or a date? Why did you do so? What impact did your attitude have on your behavior and therefore on the relationship?

- Living in reality is actually less work than living in a fantasy land. So if you tend toward the morally superior position, answer this question: "How is that position working against everything you want in life, especially in your relationships?"

Curing Blame (page 212)

Here are some guidelines to curing the blame problem.

- ***Become Self-Scrutinizing***—The most important solution is to actively observe your own soul for faults and weaknesses.

- —What faults and weaknesses—especially those that greatly impact your friendships and dating relationships—are you very much aware of?

—Remember that the ground is always level at the foot of the cross. What do you do to appropriately let dates and friends know that you are more concerned about your own sins than about theirs? And what are you doing about those sins?

—What will you do to become aware of your faults if, up to this point, you have chosen to remain blind to them? Whom, for instance, will you trust to speak the truth in love to you?

• *Relate to Both the Good and Bad of Your Date*—It is hard to maintain a blaming stance if you keep the good parts of your date in mind as much as you do the bad parts.

—Why is this approach not denial—and why is chronic blaming closer to denial?

—What good in a certain friend or date helps you accept the bad in her? Be specific.

—When, if ever, have you been very aware of a date or a friend accepting the bad as well as the good in you? How did you know about that person's awareness of your bad? How does being accepted despite your bad strengthen a relationship?

- *Set Boundaries Instead of Blaming*—Many times people blame because it is the only way they can protest what the other person is doing. It is much more helpful to confront your date in love, let him know what you will not tolerate, and set limits if the behavior continues.

—Think about a dating relationship or friendship where you were the "blamee." What boundaries could the blamer have been working on setting instead of merely blaming you?

—When, if ever, have you found it easier to blame instead of set boundaries? Be specific about the dynamics of the friendship or dating relationship.

—Blaming never really solves the problem you have. Limits often do, and thus eliminate the need for blaming in the first place. When, if ever, have you experienced or seen limits solve a problem in a dating relationship or friendship? Be specific about the work of setting boundaries and how those boundaries were received.

- *Forgive*—Another reason people continually blame is that they have difficulty forgiving their date. Forgiveness is canceling a debt that someone owes.

—When, if ever, have you felt blamed rather than forgiven? What impact did that have on the relationship?

—When, if ever, have you chosen to blame rather than to forgive? Why did you make that choice and what were the results of your decision?

—Our advice is to set limits on what can change and forgive what will not. In what current relationship, dating or otherwise, do you have an opportunity to forgive? Make it a topic of prayer and action.

- *Grieve*—While forgiveness is objective in nature, grief is its emotional component. When we cancel a debt, we are letting go of the right to demand revenge. That letting go brings loss and a feeling of sadness.

—When, if ever, have you lost the battle for a person to change, to see things your way, or to understand just how much she hurt you? What did you do with your anger at that loss—hold on to it or let go of it and grieve? What impact did your choice have on the relationship?

—Every day God lets go and feels sad about how we choose to conduct our lives (Matthew 23:37). What does this truth help you see about yourself and about how God would have you treat other people?

The five steps for curing blame which we just walked through involve some work, but they will effectively set limits on the negative power of blame in your relationship.

Before You Close the Book . . .

• Which take-away tip on pages 214–15 do you most need to take away?

Lord God, I can't do by myself the things I've read about in this chapter. Even though blame can kill a dating relationship or friendship, it's a much easier option. But I want to choose what's right, not what's easy. So in my relationships please help me be more concerned about being honest than "good," more concerned about my own sinfulness than my date's or my friend's. Help me also to humbly listen to correction and grow from it and to forgive as you have forgiven me. In Jesus' name. Amen.

Part Four

SOLVING DATING PROBLEMS:
WHEN YOUR DATE IS THE PROBLEM

Chapter 15

Say No to Disrespect

*R*emember *how Craig flirted with girls even when Cindy was by his side? The worst part of it was Craig's disregard for Cindy's discomfort with his flirting. Had he shown some concern for her feelings, she would have been less bothered by the flirting itself. The two finally broke up. Cindy couldn't see being married to someone who was great when they agreed, but ran over her feelings when they didn't.*

Dissing Is a Problem (page 221)

"Dissing" means "disrespecting," and it refers to the practice of being overly critical about someone not just behind that person's back, but also directly with that person. In the dating world, dissing is the problem of disrespecting one's dating partner. Disrespect is a serious obstacle to closeness, intimacy, and a couple's chances for marital success.

- Empathy is the ability to feel another's experience, especially painful ones. Respect is the ability to value another's experience. Any relationship needs both to be hand-in-hand.

—Respect is not worship. It has more to do with being treated as you would like to be treated, which is Jesus' Golden Rule (Matthew 7:12). What do you do or not do to show your respect for a friend or a date? Be specific. What behaviors in a friend or a date show you that he or she respects you? Again, be specific.

—Think about friendships and dating relationships. What behaviors, if any, have made you feel disrespected?

• Now think about disrespect from the other perspective. What disrespectful behaviors, if any, might you be guilty of in a dating relationship (past or present) or a friendship? The list of actions that show respect (page 222) might help you see where you may fall short.

How Disrespect Happens (page 223)

Disrespect flourishes when someone values their own desires above their date's. The other person's feelings, freedom, or needs get trampled or ignored because of how intent their date is on having their own way. Disrespect tends to be more self-centered than malicious.

• People in dating situations need to know that their feelings, needs, and freedom are respected. And disrespect usually involves some violation of freedom.

—Review the list of ways that disrespect may come out (pages 223–24). When, if ever, have you felt dominated, manipulated, violated, minimized, or blamed? When, if ever, has the person you've dated or befriended withdrawn or denied responsibility for whatever caused the problem? In each case you've identified, what freedom of yours was being violated?

—Now look in the mirror. When, if ever, have you dominated, manipulated, violated, minimized, or blamed a date? When, if ever, have you withdrawn or denied responsibility for whatever caused the problem? In each case you've identified, what freedom were you violating?

- Respecting someone doesn't mean that you agree with them. Nor does it mean that you will comply with what they want. It means that their feelings matter because those emotions belong to a person who matters.

—What encouragement do you find in Margaret and Mike's dating experience? What did you learn from their example?

—If your feelings, time, opinion, or values are not being respected, you need to take some sort of action. What current situation, if any, calls for what kind of action on your part? What might you do? Whose support can you rely on as you deal with the situation?

The Progression of Disrespect (page 225)

We aren't born respecting others. Instead, we begin life highly concerned with our own lives and hardly aware of the needs of others. Over time, we are supposed to learn that others' needs and feelings are important. But this is a learned ability, not an innate one.

- Respectful people don't lose respect over time. Instead, their respect of others increases. When has this been true for you? Explain why your respect for a person increased over time.

- What does the apparent loss of respect suggest about the person who suddenly seems more disrespectful?

If you notice disrespect increasing, you are probably instead seeing something that was hidden beginning to manifest itself. People who seem to stop respecting you over time, in all likelihood, have never had true respect for your needs and feelings.

Saying and Doing (page 226)

Another important aspect of disrespect is that it is about what we do, not what we say we will do.

- When in your experience have a person's words and promises been respectful but the follow-up actions disrespectful? And when have your words and promises been respectful but your follow-up actions disrespectful?

- It is not disrespectful to fail. It is, however, disrespectful to continually fail in an area that hurts another and not take steps to resolve the failure. In what current relationship, if any, is this truth a wake-up call for you?

What Does Not Cure Disrespect (page 227)

A disrespectful relationship has ultimately to do with character. Here are some things that will not cure a pattern of disrespect.

- Briefly note why each of the following options is not helpful:

—Ending the Relationship Immediately:

—Compliance:

—Retaliation:

—Complaining without Consequences:

What Does Cure Disrespect (page 229)

If you are experiencing a disrespectful dating relationship, here are a few action points which can go a long way toward resolving it.

- Briefly note why each of the following points is a wise move.

—Don't Wait to Deal with It:

—Get to Know Your Date in the Context of Other Relationships:

—Say No:

—Address the Disrespect as a Problem:

—Clarify:

—Bring Others In:

—Own Your Own Part:

- Now, in the space provided, tailor each point to your situation by explaining what you'll do and when.

—Don't Wait to Deal with It:

—Get to Know Your Date in the Context of Other Relationships:

—Say No:

—Address the Disrespect as a Problem:

—Clarify:

—Bring Others In:

—Own Your Own Part:

In curing disrespect, change what you need to change, but require that your date treat you respectfully. In our experience, when you do this, one of two things tends to happen: you get more respect from those who have it to give; and you get left by those who don't have it. Both results are good ones.

Before You Close the Book . . .

• Which take-away tip on page 232 do you most need to take away?

> Loving and wise God, once again I'm impressed by the profound wisdom of your Golden Rule, your command to treat others the way I want to be treated. How obedience on everyone's part would improve relationships! But we are sinners, and I'm including myself in that statement. Please forgive me when I am disrespectful—and help heal and build my character. I also ask that you would help me be wise and bold when I am being disrespected. In Jesus' name. Amen.

Chapter 16

Nip It in the Bud

*T*he issue in Mary and Todd's relationship was not an uncommon one. Todd was and always had been allowed to take advantage of other people's niceness and to not be responsible to the relationship

- What had nice Mary done to contribute to Todd's pattern of inconsiderateness?

- In relationships, you get what you tolerate. Mary's relationship with Todd illustrated this truth. When has this truth been played out for you either in your own relationship or in one you've witnessed? Be specific about what was tolerated and what in turn was gotten.

Again, in the world of dating, you will get what you tolerate. And if you are like Mary, you will get enough of it that you cannot tolerate any more, and then you will be alone again.

A Better Way (page 235)

The better way is to set your limits early on. Make them clear. Enforce them and stick to them. In short, nip it—whatever the problem is—in the bud and do not allow that weed to grow in the garden of your relationships.

• We often see situations more clearly looking back at them than we do when we are living them. So take a minute to look back. What past dating relationship (ideally yours but someone else's experience will do) would have gone more smoothly if a behavior had been nipped in the bud? Be specific about the behavior and how early on it could have been addressed.

• Why is sooner rather than later a better time to set limits to another person's behavior?

Setting the tone early in how you expect to be treated will weed out the selfish people, discipline the sloppy ones, and show your date that you have self-respect and will not tolerate being treated poorly.

Some Weeds Worth Confronting (page 235)

Patience and the ability to overlook some offenses are wonderful qualities (Proverbs 19:11), but overlooking certain negative character patterns long-term can lead to a real problem.

• Review the list of some things that should not be tolerated for very long (page 236).

—When have you tolerated any of this? At this point of *Boundaries in Dating*, what would you do differently in that situation?

—When have you been guilty of these behaviors, if any? What does that fact tell you about the growing up you need to do—and what steps will you take toward a more godly and mature character?

- Imagine facing a behavior that you should not tolerate. Review now what you would say and do to nip it in the bud. What consequences would you establish to back up what you said? Who could you count on to support your healthy action?

Set your limits and stick to them. Tell the person that you won't tolerate certain things and if they continue, he or she cannot see you until they learn how to not act that way. When you do this early, you don't yet have a lot to lose.

Short Accounts (page 236)

The best accounts are short ones (Ephesians 4:25–27). The truth of saying what bothers you is the best policy. But say it in love without sinning yourself.

- What evil can happen in ourselves and in a relationship when we aren't loving and quick with our honesty?

- What misery would you have avoided in your life if you had been loving but told the truth? And what misery would you have avoided if someone had lovingly told you the truth early on? Be specific—and let this experience spur you on to quick and loving honesty the next time.

Nip intolerable behavior fast. You will either chase off a bad person or make sure a good one does not slip into one.

Before You Close the Book . . .

- Which take-away tip on page 237 do you most need to take away?

Lord God, again I see the wisdom of your eternal principles for the nitty-gritty of daily life. Make me, I pray, a person of integrity and love who speaks and lives truth. Make me also a person who can hear truth and act on it, turning to you for growth and change. Give me courage and wisdom to confront things that are important and the grace to forgive and tolerate when that is appropriate. May I live out my dating relationships in the light of truth. In Jesus' name. Amen.

Chapter 17

Set Appropriate Physical Limits

Jenny and Dave's situation may be all too familiar to you. And you may have several of the same questions people who are dating and falling in love ask about physical limits.

- Which of the questions on page 240 have you asked?

Let's take a look at these questions—and the answers—now.

The Big Rule, and More (page 240)

God wants people to reserve sex for marriage. But if it feels so good, and is good for the relationship, and both people are consenting, then what is the problem?

- What value have you recognized in God's rule because of experiences (yours and other people's) in dating and the single life?

- If you haven't carefully read 1 Thessalonians 4:3–8 yet, do so now (page 241). Circle or underline phrases which give the reasons for God's rule.

Now we'll look at each of the reasons God calls for sexual abstinence outside marriage.

Holy and Honorable (page 241)

Paul calls God's people to "control [their] body in a way that is holy and honorable"
(1 Thessalonians 4:4). "Holiness" means purity and being set aside for a high purpose, and
"honor" means things like "dignity, precious, of high price or value, or high esteem." So, first,
God is saying that sex is not a casual thing. Like other things of high value, to spend sex casu-
ally or unwisely is foolish, and you will be cheated in the end.

- Amanda's breakup experience was very different from the man who had also thought
  he had "found the one." What point do their experiences illustrate?

- Amanda felt as if she had lost a part of herself when Monte left. Why? Because sex
  and the heart are connected. Why do so many of us learn that the hard way—from
  experience rather than from people who have gone before us?

The first lesson here is that sex is set apart for a purpose and has great value. It is for
a lifelong commitment and needs to be esteemed. In a physical and spiritual sense, it is all
you can give someone. Therefore, it should not be given away lightly.

Self-Control (page 243)

Paul says, "Each of you should learn to control his own body" (1 Thessalonians 4:4). Con-
trol of one's own body is a sign that a person is capable of delay of gratification and self-
control, which are prerequisites of the ability to love.

- If someone is able to respect the limit of hearing no for sex, that is a character sign
  of someone who can say no to their own desires and hungers in order to serve a higher
  purpose, or to love another person. When, if at all, have you seen this truth—or
  its converse—illustrated in real life, in your experience or in someone else's?

- A committed relationship calls for sacrifice.

—In friendships as well as dating relationships, what kinds of sacrifices have you seen made—or perhaps made yourself—in any of the following areas?

Time

Money

Getting one's own way

Working out conflict

—What kind of sacrifices are involved in respecting boundaries about sex?

- What is a good response to "If you love me, you will [have sex]"?

Choose someone who can delay gratification for the sake of you and the relationship. Boundaries with sex are a sure-fire test to know if someone loves you for you.

Passionate Lust (page 246)

Paul also teaches against passionate lust (1 Thessalonians 4:5), against a lust for that which is forbidden outside of marriage.

- A healthy person is someone who is integrated: the body, the soul, and the mind are all working together. If someone has not married you, then they have given less than 100 percent of themselves and should get less than 100 percent of your body.

—"Lusters" have divided souls and do not develop deeper aspects of themselves which are necessary for a lasting relationship. What undeveloped skills can sex outside of marriage keep a person from dealing with? What activities can sex replace?

—When, if ever, have you seen sex during dating hide a person's lack of relational skills? What happened to the people involved?

Instead of expressing love through sex, the luster replaces love with sex.

- Your sexual abstinence is a great way to find out how fulfilled you are as a person.

—When, if ever, have you used sex to replace relationship? What does that action tell you about your deep longings and unhealed hurts? Some things that may be driving your passionate lust are listed on page 249.

—What lesson do you learn from Sally's experience? What encouragement do you find in her story?

Passionate lust splits you from your real heart, your mind, your values, and the life that you truly desire. Lust gets momentary fulfillment at the expense of lasting gain. Furthermore—as countless married women have found out—the person they married who could not wait was incapable of real relationship.

Wronging Someone (page 250)

Paul also teaches that when sex occurs outside of marriage, someone is always wronged (1 Thessalonians 4:6). When someone sleeps with a person whom he or she is not married to, he or she is hurting that person.

- Why is the action hurtful? Review the eight reasons listed on pages 250–51. If you have slept with someone outside of marriage, note which hurts you experienced as a result.

- If you have pressured someone to sleep with you outside of marriage, what hurts listed might you have inflicted? What, if anything, have you done to seek forgiveness—God's as well as that person's?

If you say that you are a person of love, then you won't wrong someone you love. You will wait. And vice versa, do not allow anyone else to wrong you. Love waits to give, but lust can't wait to get.

Accepting God (page 251)

Finally, Paul teaches us that the authority for sexuality belongs not to us, but to God. And there are few better tests for whether or not someone lives a life in submission to God than what he or she does with their sexuality.

- Why is it important—for a dating relationship now and for a possible marriage in the future—to see whether a person submits to the Lord? Put differently, what kinds of problems will arise if your date "submits" only when God's way doesn't interfere with his or her desires?

- What does the litmus test of your sexuality tell you about yourself, your spirituality, and your submission to the God of the Bible rather than to a God you're recreating to fit your needs and desires? Are you walking humbly with your God (Micah 6:8)? What repentance is in order?

God wants to be accepted as he really is, rules and all. When someone rewrites his values, they are not accepting who he really is. So be sure you're trusting a person who truly trusts God. If he or she is, that person will uphold God's value of sex within marriage.

Reminders of Reasons to Say No (page 253)

Sexuality is a part of God's good creation. But, as you embrace your sexuality, do so with self-control, sanctity, high esteem, lovingly and not lustfully, sacrificially and not "wronging" someone, and in submission to God.

- What freedom comes with following God's law specifically in the area of sexuality?

- Look at the checklist of things you can learn if you say no to sex outside of marriage (pages 253–54). What are some of the benefits that come with holding your ground?

It is difficult to keep someone out of your heart who has invaded your body. That in itself is another reason to say no to sex outside of marriage.

The Boundary of Forgiveness (page 254)

Angie didn't understand how God looks at our failures. Do you?

- "Once I made a mistake," Angie remembers, "I thought that I had already blown it. I had not saved myself for that one person whom I would give my life to. So, with the next boyfriend, and the ones after him, I thought, *What's the difference? I already blew it.*"

—What truth about God's forgiveness could you offer to someone who feels like Angie does? (That someone may be yourself.)

—Support your point with one or more of the following passages: Psalm 103:12; Romans 8.1, Hebrews 10:17, 22; and 1 John 1:0.

• Your past failure does not have to doom you to further sexual brokenness. You can become clean again. You can become pure again.

—What further hope do the last four paragraphs of this chapter (pages 255–56) offer you? Which truths are especially meaningful and encouraging to you?

—Who can help you stay on the path of purity? Be sure to build a support system if one is not already in place.

Dating can be a place of growth instead of brokenness. And when you accept forgiveness through Jesus and walk, cleansed, in a state of being guilt-free, you'll find it a strong state indeed. And then you can wait on the real thing.

Before You Close the Book . . .

- Which take-away tip on page 256 do you most need to take away?

Almighty and Creator God, I'm understanding better than ever how your lordship is key to my sexuality. For whatever reason, I've challenged your wisdom regarding my sexuality more often than I've doubted your guidelines for honesty and respect and other dimensions of a relationship. Forgive me for that pride, for that refusal to submit. And forgive me for the sexual brokenness I've chosen and/or caused. Please help me to receive your forgiveness and to submit to your will for me in this—and every other—area of my life. And please help me to look to you for strength as I walk the path of purity you call me to, as I save your gift and see waiting as an act of love for my future spouse. In Jesus' name. Amen.

Chapter 18

Set Up a Detention Hall

*S*olving problems of love, respect, responsibility, and commitment in dating relationships is the theme of this chapter. Though no one has the power to fix anyone else, you do have the power to respond in healthy ways to your date when problems arise. And healthy responses, which often involve the careful, caring use of boundaries, can go a long way toward a better relationship.

By the way, we'll address the "boundary bustee" rather than the boundary buster because the one who is reaping what someone else is sowing is typically more motivated to do something about the problem.

Some Conflict Is Normal (page 258)

Problems, including boundary conflicts, are a normal part of relationships.

- Why is this news to you (if it is)?

- And, news or not, what about this truth is freeing?

Give up the demand that your relationship be conflict-free, get over it, and go to the next step.

Require Boundaries in Your Relationship (page 259)

Next, don't wait to set a limit until there is a huge problem or crisis in your love life. Boundaries should be woven into the fabric of your life and relationship, as something that you do and say daily.

- Setting limits is simply about being honest about what you allow and don't allow. So let's review. What are some basics about what you allow and don't allow in a dating relationship?

- What safe places do you have to practice living out your boundaries and/or to get support for doing so in your dating life? Work on developing that support system. It's key to healthy and godly dating.

Make honesty, responsibility, respect, and freedom a required part of all aspects of your relationship: socially, emotionally, sexually, spiritually, and in every other area.

See Boundaries as Preserving the Relationship, Not Ending It (page 260)

Deal with your fear of setting limits. See boundaries as tools for diagnosing the character of your date and of the relationship.

- When have you seen boundaries reveal brokenness, character weakness, and/or unhealthy patterns? Be specific about the circumstances.

- Briefly explain why boundaries can help cure problems of irresponsibility, domination, and manipulation.

Boundary Problem Versus Character Problem (page 261)

Boundary problems are one thing. However, there is a deeper problem: the character of the person who is crossing the boundary.

- The essence of a boundary problem (and there are many [page 261]) is probably someone sowing a problem and not reaping the effects (the boundary buster), and someone else reaping what he never sowed (the boundary bustee) (Galatians 6:7). The solution is to restructure things so the sower is also the reaper.

—Give an example of boundary busting from real life—from your own experience, someone else's, or a situation you've read about in this book.

—Now outline the restructuring (boundary setting and consequence enforcing) that can help solve the problem.

- The boundary violation and the character of the person you are dating cannot be isolated from each other.

—Why is it important to keep this truth in mind if you're dealing with a boundary buster?

—If you're a boundary buster, what aspect of your character do you need to be working on? What will you do to submit your character to God's process of growth?

Love, Respect, and Mutuality (page 263)

As you think about approaching your date with the problem, adopt a stance of love, respect, and mutuality.

- Why is each of these three elements important—and how would you extend them to the boundary buster in your life?

Love

Respect

Mutuality

- As the boundary bustee, for what contributions to the situation do you need to apologize to the violator? See some possibilities on page 264.

Draw the Line (page 264)

Your best approach is to be very specific with your date about the boundary problem. Have specific events that you can draw from, what you felt when they happened, what was the problem with what happened, and what you wished had happened instead.

- Why are specifics essential to drawing the line?

- What specific character issue do you also need to address as you draw the line about a certain behavior?

Boundaries Are Not Consequences! (page 266)

Stating your boundary is not enough. You also have to lay down a consequence and stick to it. Consequences are the realities you set up for when the boundary is crossed again. They involve some sort of pain for your date. Consequences are God's school of discipline (Hebrews 12:11).

- When, if ever, have consequences helped you learn a lesson or perhaps helped you teach one to a date, friend, employee, or child? Describe the situation and the lesson learned.

- Think of a dating situation (yours or someone else's) where consequences were needed to back up the statement of a boundary. Was the consequence appropriate and effective? Why or why not? Explain.

What Is a Fitting Consequence? (page 267)

You will need to determine what an appropriate consequence is for the infractions that keep occurring. The punishment needs to fit the crime. Four principles help provide a way of thinking about what is appropriate.

- After each guideline, note the most helpful reminder from the description on pages 268–69.

—Be Motivated by Love and Truth, Not Revenge:

—Avoid the Ultimate Consequence:

—Think Empathically:

—Use Reality as Your Guide:

- Consider again the specific dating situation you described in "Boundaries Are Not Consequences!" In light of these guidelines, consider the consequences that were established. What do the guidelines suggest about the consequences? Were they fitting?

—Be Motivated by Love and Truth, Not Revenge:

—Avoid the Ultimate Consequence:

—Think Empathically:

—Use Reality as Your Guide:

Keep in mind the function of a consequence: to protect you and to help your date face the realities of his destructive pattern.

Points to Remember in Boundary Setting (page 269)

When you set boundaries, you are allowing pain to touch someone important to you. The conflict of wanting closeness, yet having to take a righteous stance with a boundary-less person, can take its toll. We've identified some things to have in place as you go through the process.

- Review the descriptions of the following (pages 269–72). What statement in each section is most helpful?

—Stay Connected:

—Avoid Reactive Friends:

—Expect Negative Reactions:

—Empathize with the Struggle:

—Be Patient:

—Question His Motives:

—Provide a Way Back to Normality: •

- You may have tried setting boundaries and establishing consequences to enforce them. If they didn't work, what does this list suggest about why?

- You may need to establish some consequences in a relationship right now. Which of the seven things do you need to work on having in place? What will you do toward that goal?

Should You Require the Growth Process? (page 272)

If you have boundary struggles with someone you are involved with, it makes sense to set up consequences aimed at dealing with the problem. But should you go further and require that your date enter some sort of process of spiritual or emotional growth? In the example we gave, we think Tina should look for spiritual growth from Brent.

- *Spiritual Growth Is Not Optional*—First, we believe that everyone needs to be involved in the process of spiritual growth. This means being in a process in which the person brings his struggles, weaknesses, and vulnerabilities to God and some safe people on an ongoing basis. As he confesses his sins and failings, he gets forgiveness, comfort, and truth to work through his issues over time, and God grows him up (Ephesians 4:16).

—How have you yourself benefited from being involved in the process of spiritual growth? Be specific. And if you haven't yet, what step will you take to get involved?

—Why is reluctance to be involved in spiritual growth a yellow flag, if not a red one?

Would you want to risk living the rest of your life with someone who is essentially disconnected from his own soul and from God? If he does not hunger and thirst for God, growth, and change above all else, you risk a lot of emptiness and misery.

- *Character Growth Cures Problems*—Second, if your date's boundary violation is a pattern, as opposed to a one-time specific event, it is likely tied to a character problem. It is best not to be satisfied if he simply stops doing the bad thing or starts doing the good thing.

—What will happen if a character problem is ignored? Put differently, how long can a change of behavior be maintained if it is not accompanied by a change in character?

—What point does the metaphor of the dry drunk reinforce?

Go for God's true process of growth and require spiritual growth as well as changes in behavior.

- **Use Limits to Test the Relationship**—Finally, insist that your boundary-busting date get into a process of spiritual growth in order to test whether you really should stay together.

—Consider the long-term effects of being with someone who isn't interested in growing spiritually. Summarize why dating is the best arena to determine a person's interest in God, growth, and change.

—Why is the call to spiritual growth an appropriate litmus test for a dating relationship?

Find someone who loves God and who you can grow with. Then enjoy the journey together!

One more word. It is our sincere hope that you now know how to approach your date and the boundary problems you may be facing. Remember that God cares deeply for both of you and has solutions for whatever issues you may face.

Before You Close the Book . . .

- Which take-away tip on page 275 do you most need to take away?

> *Lord God, I am so glad you love me and care about my dating rela-*
> *tionships! And I am so aware of how I need to keep you involved in my*
> *dating life. I need your wisdom and guidance first to choose dates and*
> *later as I deal with the conflicts that are inevitable. I need your compas-*
> *sion and strength as I establish consequences to support my boundaries.*
> *I need your people to support me in the good and the bad of dating.*
> *And I need your transforming power in my own journey of spiritual*
> *growth. Please don't let me shut you out of my dating life—and I thank*
> *you in advance for your faithfulness, your goodness, and your*
> *presence with me always. In Jesus' name. Amen.*

CONCLUSION

*B*oundaries in dating is about becoming a truthful, caring, responsible, and free person who encourages growth in those you are in contact with. We've listed six critical measures of a good dating relationship to help you make sure that the good things God has designed in dating are actually occurring.

- Review what we say about each measure and, below, write down anything you want to be sure to remember.

—Is Dating Growing Me Up?

—Is Dating Bringing Me Closer to God?

—Am I More Able to Have Good Relationships?

—Am I Picking Better Dates Over Time?

—Am I a Better Potential Mate?

—Am I Enjoying the Ride?

- Now step back and look in the mirror.

—If you've been dating, how are you doing? Where are you pleased? What points do you want to work on?

—Whether you have an active dating life or you're about to start dating, what specific goals do you have for your dating life?

—Whatever your situation, what about this book's perspective on dating has convicted you? Challenged you? Encouraged you?

In closing, we pray the Father's hand on all your dating relationships and activities. God bless you in your own boundaries and dating.

HENRY CLOUD, PH.D.
JOHN TOWNSEND, PH.D.

For information on books, resources or speaking engagements:

Cloud-Townsend Resources
3176 Pullman Avenue, Suite 104
Costa Mesa, CA 92626
Phone: 1-800-676-HOPE (4673)
Web: www.cloudtownsend.com

We want to hear from you. Please send your comments about this
book to us in care of the address below. Thank you.

ZondervanPublishingHouse
Grand Rapids, Michigan 49530
http://www.zondervan.com